THE BOOK OF MATRIXING

The science behind the Martial Arts
(book one in the Matrixing/Neutronics series)

Al Case

copyright©2024 by Alton H. Case

The Book of the Matrixing is a compilation of the following three books:

Martial Arts 101: Fixing the Martial Arts

The Science of Matrixing in the Martial Arts

Binary Matrixing in the Martial Arts

All of which were previously published by Quality Press.

For information regarding matrixing:

MonsterMartialArts. com

TABLE OF CONTENTS

Martial Arts 101:
Fixing the Martial Arts

TABLE OF CONTENTS FOR MATRIXING 101

COMPLETE LIST OF BOOKS AND VIDEOS BY AL CASE

MARTIAL ARTS

How to Create Kenpo 1
How to Create Kenpo 2
How to Create Kenpo 3
Pan Gai Noon Karate/Kung Fu
Kang Duk Won Korean Karate
Kwon Bup American Karate
Outlaw Karate
Buddha Crane Karate
Karate to Shaolin to Pa Kua Chang
Matrixing Tong Bei
Fixing MCMAP 1
Fixing MCMAP 2
Bruce Lee vs Classical Martial Arts
Shaolin Butterfly
Butterfly Pa Kua Chang
The Hardest Punch in the World
How to be a Master Instructor
Matrix Karate: White Belt
Matrix Karate: Green Belt
Matrix Karate: Brown Belt
Matrix Karate: Black Belt
Matrix Karate: Master
Binary Matrixing
How to Matrix the Martial Arts
The Master Text
How to Matrix Kick Boxing
Monkey Boxing Forms
Matrixing Chi
Chiang Nan

Cogswell
Yoga
Yogata: The Yoga Kata
Black Belt Yoga

Children
Universal Glue
Return of the Dragon

NOVELS

Spreadwing
Grave Business
The North Mansion
The Haunting of House
Machina
Monkeyland
The Bomber's Story 1 & 2
The Lone Star Revolt
Yancy
Return to Monkeyland
Small in the Saddle
When the Cold Wind Blows
Path of the Snake
Path of the Wizard
Path of the Dragon
Twisted Gods
Hero
Assassin
Avatar
Falling Skies
Pack
Fugue
The Mortal Coil
Ethereal Bodyguard
The Day They Bombed LA
Day the President Killed the US
Light Insane Yogi Eyeballs
How to Kill
Curse of the Gods
Transformation of George

Lobo Love
Lobo University
The Naked Witch
15th Chapter
Little Girls

Introduction

When I began the martial arts I really had no idea where I was going, but I did know one thing: I wanted everything to make sense.

In the world of the martial arts this is difficult.

Systems are combined, concepts overlap, people put stuff together out of whim and profit…it makes no sense.

The interesting thing is that, even though it makes no sense, it works. The martial arts cause a human being to evolve, to become enlightened, to become a better, more advanced person.

The only problem is that it takes…so…long!

So I created matrixing, isolated the arts and put them back together, and the path became so…much…faster.

And, the path became more than just learning to fight; more than just getting a black belt.

The path became one of self-betterment, enlightenment, living a long and fruitful life, free from the distractions and dissipations that plague ordinary citizens.

Learn an art.

Matrix that art.

Matrix all the arts.

Apply matrixing to other areas.

Discover your humanity and share it.

It's a simple solution, but it's like a drop of dye in the ocean. The fact is that the ordinary citizen is rapidly declining in intelligence, health and spirituality.

We have just have too many conventions that are harmful: government education, pharmafoods, drugs, out of control electronics.

The result is that people buy what they've been told, eat what is placed before them, look to drugs and electronics for fun, and don't understand how this makes them…well, stupid.

And the government, being a beneficiary of all this silliness, is certainly not going to do anything about it.

No, the only people who are going to do anything about the sad state of mankind is the individual. That unique person who has the fortitude and willpower to stand against what is popular and do what is right.

If you are studying the martial arts, then you are on the path of that unique individual. But you have to study the corrected martial arts. Not the abuse that has been created by man for self glory and domination.

This book will help you fix the martial arts; it will offer you the exact data to make your martial arts better and superior.

Hopefully your interest will be piqued, and you will look into matrixing, and proceed from there.

In this book I go through the basics, through the problems with techniques and forms…and entire systems. I do this with 101 unique chapters.

If you are a previous student of mine you may have seen some of the material in this book.

And, the courses I have written on matrixing, specifically matric karate and the Master Instructor course, are the last word, and senior to this book. On those courses I don't just tell…I show, and in the time since I published those courses, and the others on MonsterMartialArts.com, nobody has ever disproved them.

You simply can't argue with the physics of the universe, especially physics that have been expanded by Matrixing.

At any rate, in this book I go all the way through, to the end of the martial arts, and discuss what things are at the end of the martial path.

I am reminded of the allegory of the cave.

Mankind lives in a vast cavern. In the center of the cavern is a huge fire. On the walls of the cavern play the sick and twisted flames and shadows of the people in the cave.

Some people feed the fire, and tell you what the shadows mean, feeding you myth and fantasy, enjoying being such important people.

A few people, literally one in millions, tell you the way out of the cavern.

The 'authorities,' the ones fanning the flames, call that one person a liar, and try to rouse the people against him.

Understand this and you understand that the martial arts are in a cave…and if you can put aside the myth and fantasy in the martial arts you can put aside the myth and fantasy in the larger cave, the one that holds all humanity.

So, here you are, possessing the truth of your existence.

What will you do now?

Al Case

Chapter One
Don't Be a Know It All

The first thing to be stated, and to be taken in and learned, certainly to be adhered to, is that the reader must not flip the pages of this book as a 'know it all.'

Empty your cup, put aside previous teachings, and consider my words apart from the art.

Then put them into the art. Fresh. Unhindered by previous observations.

Once upon a time I wrote a book, a darned good book, and the first person to buy it offered a scathing review. He judged my book, and me, in terrible lights. Excoriated me.

And all under the umbrella of his 10 years in the martial arts.

Book didn't sell well, even though I had excellent reviews on certain portions of the book which had appeared earlier as articles.

Simply, people were impressed by his authority, and didn't take the time to consider that I was speaking from the viewpoint of 50 years experience.

A beginner, a mere black belt, compared to 5 decades in the martial arts. Decades that were filled with writing for the mags, producing training videos, writing MILLIONS of words on the subject.

Now, here's the thing: this fellow, with his limited experience, used my book to establish himself as authority. To make himself look good.

He had never written a book, he had only studied one art, he had no facts on what I do, which included my inclusion of Matrixing logic in the construction of the book and description of the art.

He had only opinion.

And thus my book waits in the dust bins for nothing but ever increasing obscurity.

One guy was a know it all, and deprived all other martial artists, of valuable data that would have changed their art.

So I tell you this, whether you have a day or a decade of experience, Consider my words fresh.

Divest yourself of opinion before the fact, of improper teachings (which will become obvious as you enter into the book), and try out my words.

Take my words out on to the mat and ascertain for yourself whether I make sense or not.

Trust yourself, not some bozo wallowing in insecurity.

Chapter Two
Stand Squarely in the Room

There is an old Japanese saying in the martial arts: 'Stand squarely in the room.'

This is an important point, and should be understood with your first lessons in the martial arts.

Power, you see, is your ability to hold a position.

To establish yourself as real, or at least responsible for some portion of the universe.

This saying translates into a simple fact of action: be able to move in any direction without 'pre-leaning.'

The simple fact is that all too often people will lean in a direction before they move; they unbalance themselves to achieve motion.

This is amazingly inefficient.

The purposes of the legs are twofold, with a minor third purpose.

First: to grab the planet with the feet so as not to be able to be moved.

Second: to launch oneself into motion across the face of the planet.

A minor third: kicks.

These actions, ground, move and kick, require balance, and standing squarely in the room speaks to balance.

You should apply this principle, indeed, this philosophy, into your every motion. Be it form or freestyle, or even dancing or rock climbing: 'Stand squarely, assume a firm position that is in balance.

Your ability to move will be logically and scientifically enhanced.

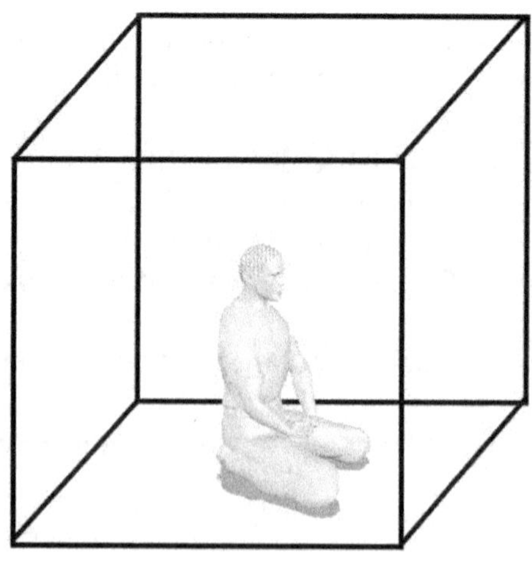

Chapter Three
Walk with the Feet Straight

A lot of people are getting knee replacements, hip replacements, and that sort of thing.

Unfortunately, even unbelievably, some of these people are martial artists.

So why didn't the martial arts protect these people from the wearing down of their bodies?

Because they were doing the martial arts wrong. They were doing them so wrong they actually contributed to the malfunctioning of their bodies.

Take a look at the bottom of your shoe.

Is the heel worn down on one side or the other? That is called 'pronation.' That means you have been walking wrong.

The correct way to walk is to place the heel gently and roll, utilizing the arch as spring.

Listen to people walk. Sometimes you hear them slapping the ground, deliberately abusing their feet.

Watch people walk. Sometimes you see them walking with the feet pointed out, or in, which deliberately abuses the ankles, the knees, even the hips and backbone.

The correct way to walk is silently, like a cat, rolling the arch as described.

If you don't walk this way you wear the heels (pronate) which results in compensation by the knees, which results in compensation by the hips, which results in compensation by the backbone.

The trick, of course, is going to be in applying this principle to your martial arts.

To examine your stances, the way you move the foot, the turn of the ankle and rotation of the joint.

Examine the whole body, but starting with the feet, and find the correct way of using each joint.

Ball and socket? Hinge? On which sides of the joint are the muscles? How do the joints act in relation to one another?

This is the way to move your body move most efficiently, and without causing yourself damage.

This is the way to make your motions smoother and more efficient.

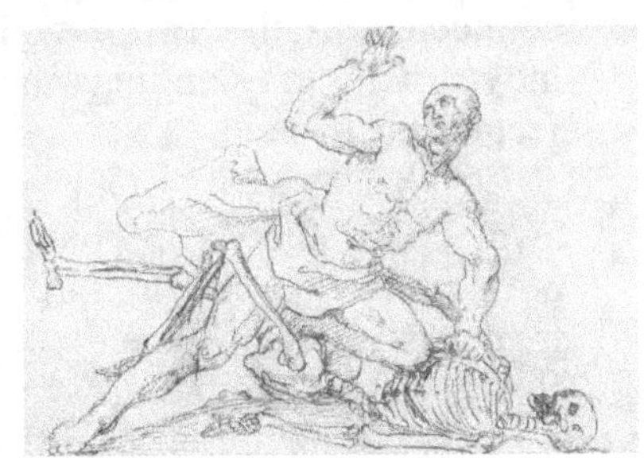

Chapter Four
Bouncing Versus Grounding

Bouncing is a boxing thing. We didn't used to bounce when I was learning the martial arts in the late 60s. Bouncing came in first with Bruce Lee, who was doubtless influenced by boxing, and then by boxing itself.

Bouncing isn't bad if you are working on cardio, but it is opposed to the purposes of the feet.

If you are bouncing then you are not grounding, which means you are not sinking your weight, which means you are not standing squarely in the room.

When I engage in freestyle with a bouncer I find it very easy to gage the height of the bounce, and launch myself (2nd purpose of the legs) when they are at the top of their bounce. This means that I will be covering distance towards them while they are still in the air.

A good way of understanding this is when somebody does a jump kick, they are locked in trajectory till they reach the ground. This gives you all sorts of time in which to maneuver, set up a trap, etc.

The fact of the matter is that one can maneuver around an opponent with the feet connected, or 'grounded,' and do so much more efficiently than when bouncing.

The sad fact of the matter is that when bouncing came into vogue, way back in the 60s and early 70s, most people didn't understand how to keep the feet grounded while moving, to ground from foot to foot smoothly so one was never off balance, so bouncing appeared more efficient.

And, courtesy of Bruce, it was so cool looking.

I probably wouldn't have learned if I hadn't spent a few years doing Pa Kua Chang.

But you can learn in any art if you just remember to keep balanced, stay connected to the earth, and move without slapping the feet on the ground.

It is hard, takes awareness, and is probably not as fun as bouncing, but it is more efficient when you finally learn how to do it.

Chapter Five
The Purpose of Stretching

There is the obvious purpose of increasing flexibility, and one does well even if they just strive for flexibility. Flexibility aids the body in motion, forestalls injury, and keeps you healthy. However, there is a deeper purpose here.

When one enters into a stretch the body has a knee-jerk reaction to tighten up. The body just is afraid it will stretch too far, 'come apart,' as it were.

The good martial artist should do the stretch only until there is initial tightening of the muscle. Only until the muscle says ''Whoa!' and starts to tighten.

Don't force it at that point, rather relax it.

Hold that position and mentally tell the muscle to relax.

Slowly, the muscle will relax, get over the idea that you're going to rip the body in two, and the 'hint' of pain will go away.

Thus, you use stretching as a feedback device to learn how to relax, and that is the underlying purpose here.

You want a healthy, flexible body.

But you don't want to go through pain to make it happen.

You want to go through relaxation.

Much more efficient, causes MUCH less injury.

It is usually slower, that is for sure, but that is okay.

Slow and sure wins the race...and avoids a few months waiting for tissue to repair.

Learn to relax and you will be MUCH more capable of motion. And speed and quickness and so on.

You may run out of muscle, which means you may run out of rigidity, but you will never run out of emptiness, which is to say...relaxation.

This is why stretches should be at the beginning of any class, not to make the body flexible, but to make it relax so that it can be flexible.

Can you Relax
When you Stretch?

Chapter Six
The Purpose of Stances

This is a dichotomous universe, which is to say that it is a motor, and tension between the two sides of the motor keeps it in existence.

This is analogous to the purpose of stances.

When one assumes a stance one is creating a motor with the earth; the earth is one terminal and the body is the other. Using this motor one can increase physical strength, and even increase the commodity known as 'chi.'

The formula to describe this is:

Weight = Work = Energy

The deeper the stance, the harder one has to work, the more energy one uses…and creates.

This energy can be used to ground a person, which means to connect the body to the ground, or to launch a person.

There are three types of stances:

one leg grounded
the other leg grounded
both legs grounded

The study of stances is a study in how to move from one grounded position to the next. One should be able to move in any direction, into any stance.

While classical studies teach this, a thorough understanding can be had by matrixing stances.

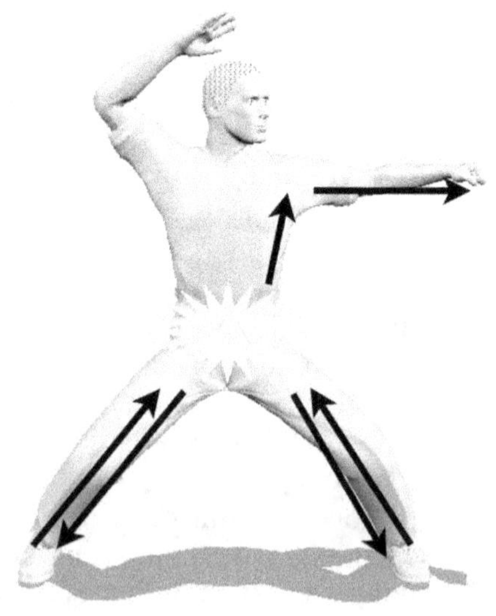

The deeper you sink,
The more power you have!

Chapter Seven
The Horse Stance

The easiest way to learn the truth of stances, and of the self, is to simply do a Horse Stance for an hour.

After a couple of years of training I decided to do this. The instructors at the Kang Duk Won could hold their stances, deep ones, for over an hour, shouldn't I learn from them?

So thinking, I began one night.

I first decided to hold my horse stance through television commercials. A commercial is only a minute. Surely I could last through a couple of commercials?

Never have commercials been so long.

After a couple of weeks I was able to do this pretty easily.

Then I had an idea: why don't I just do it?

After all, I had managed to ignore pain for a couple of minutes at a time…why not just ignore pain all together and just do it?

So I began.

My legs trembled. Sweat burst out on my face. The pain began.

I ignored it. It was only pain, after all…it wasn't like standing in a horse stance was going to kill me, right?

After five minutes the pain stopped.

Totally stopped.

I mean, it just went away and wasn't.

Pain was gone and I stood like a golden buddha on top of a mountain.

I realized I could stay like this forever.

I had put aside the physical universe in the form of pain, and I was now in the ethereal. I was spirit, and I controlled matter.

So what did it matter?

A while later I decided to come back to earth.

Except…I couldn't move!

I was frozen, locked in place!

I began to lurch forward and back, at first in my mind, and then my body began to shift minutely.

I toppled, and I was so locked up that I couldn't even move my arms.

I landed, face first, on the living room floor.

50 years of horse meditation

Probably the first person in history to knock himself out doing the Horse Stance.

Chapter Eight
Tension in the Stance

One should build tension in a stance if they want to effectively push against the earth (to launch the body).

Take a stance, bend the knees and sink the weight.

Shift forward slightly and the front leg loads the weight and becomes the coiled spring.

Shift backward slightly and the back leg loads the weight and becomes the coupled spring.

When you want to move, simply lift the leg that is not coiled, the 'bracing' leg, as it were, and let the 'coiled spring' leg launch the body.

Practicing this simple move will enable one to spurt forward with extreme quickness.

This move encourages shuffling, which is a move not practiced in any form, yet extremely valuable in freestyle.

To practice this in the horse stance I used to take a horse stance sideways to a wall. I would place one hand against a wall and grab the inner foot with my outer hand. I would then practice breathing slowly, and imagine an arc of energy going through my body from the floor to the wall.

You can practice this type of method with any stance, even holding yourself up with blocks or punches out of the various stances.

You can practice imagining arcs and lines of energy through your body in forms, with kicks, just about any move there is.

I particularly enjoyed imagining an arc of energy through a posture, then imagining it warping into another posture.

One hand against the wall,
Energy runs from wall to floor.

Chapter Nine
Splaying the Horse

This is one of my favorite ones when I want to point out silliness in the martial arts. The thing is, this is a favorite posture of a major martial art, and attested to by instructors and masters.

In Goju there is a 'splayed-foot' Horse Stance. This is a horse stance with the feet pointed outwards, like a duck.

You see pictures of masters in the stance, yet you never see it working, and nobody talks about the function, except in the most arcane and mystical sense.

One explanation for it was that it 'softened the back.'

Wha…?

Why would you want to soften the back?

The fact of the matter is that pointing the feet outward causes the hips to tilt the wrong way.

The hips should not tilt forward, but rather be tucked. This strengthens the back, and the back even seems to send nerve impulses more efficiently like this.

Certainly the weight = work = energy formula works better.

Try it yourself, if you don't believe.

But more: the muscles in the body should align in supportive directions. These usually means in the same directions. If you take a splayed-foot horse stance you are pointing the legs in different directions, pointing the muscles in different directions, and this opposes, almost directly, the idea of the purpose of the legs (ground or move).

And, if you really examine the concept and posture, you are opposing the idea of a motor with the 'splayed-foot' stance.

And, under it all, this tends to split intention. A definite no no, as you will see when we discuss such things as intention.

Splayed feet causes lower back to curve,
which causes weakness in the back.

Chapter Ten
Shuffling

I have mentioned, earlier in this book, that the shuffle is very abused. Or…not used.

I had a student who went to a tournament. He matched up against a Japanese stylist and began hitting the fellow. Unfortunately, they wouldn't give him any points. Again and again he scored, and I saw what was happening.

Being a Japanese style tournament, they believed that only a strike from a front stance was valid. My student was shuffling in and striking out of a back stance.

And, in the end, the other fellow, after being struck a dozen times, managed to get one front stance punch in.

Now, there is nothing wrong with striking out of a front stance. You are thrusting your whole weight into the punch.

But isn't a shuffling back stance using the whole weight?

And, here's the trick, isn't a shuffling back stance thrusting the whole weight…without being limited by nailing down the back foot?

Now forms use stepping. I believe only Hsing I truly utilizes the shuffle movement.

Isn't that interesting that almost the whole martial arts has left out the shuffle?

And it is probably because, when the Okinawan masters agreed in secret pact to not teach the martial arts, and they began teaching 'behavior modification' karate to school children, it was easier to teach the children to step instead of shuffle.

At any rate, if you shuffle forward you lift the front foot slightly, releasing the coiled spring of the back leg, and launch forward, dragging the back leg and setting down in a back stance. Or whatever stance you wish.

If you shuffle backward you lift the back leg, the front leg is the coiled spring, and you launch backwards, dragging the front leg after.

You should be able to do any kick, block or strike with the shuffle.

THE SHUFFLE!

From a back stance…

lift the front foot as you…

push with the rear foot…

then drag the rear foot forward.

Chapter Eleven
The Front Stance

Read an instruction book on the martial arts and you will frequently come across the advice that when in a front stance your weight is 70/30, or 60/40, or some other math.

I remember reading about a Tai Chi instructor who got curious, broke out two bathroom scales, and proved the idea false.

That said, the front shin, in a front stance, should be up and down. If you have it straight it can be kicked and the leg broken. If it goes too far forward, say beyond the toes, the knee hurts.

The back leg should always be bent slightly. Even if you have thrust your weight forward to an extreme, there must be a slight coil available for a further push in the forward direction.

The hips, when using the arm on the front leg side, should be in alignment with the line of the feet, and the shoulders.

When using the arm on the back leg side the hips should be squared.

This is all easily tested for efficiency simply by pushing or pulling on the blocks or strikes.

Whether pushing or pulling, the stance should be balanced (squarely in the room), and the energy should go up/down the appropriate leg (rear leg for a front push/back pull, front leg for a front pull/back push.

You can set up and test any stance according to the things I tell you here.

You should make your stance perfect, then explore how to keep them perfect through the moves of a form.

Front shin straight up and down.

Back leg slightly curved.

Hips, shoulders and feet in common line (curve).

Chapter Twelve
The Back Stance

Most people don't understand the back stance at all.

They either 'brace' it against the ground (I did, in the beginning) making it inadequate for launching the body. Yet emphasizing the back leg as the coiled spring reveals the purpose of the stance as a launch platform.

So you have to bend as in squatting, not just bend and brace against the ground.

The Japanese, especially Shotokan, have been very misled in this matter. If you study their back stance the back foot is turned outward. Thus, the stance is actually a combination of horse and back stances, which none of the strengths of both stances, and some of the weaknesses.

For instance, the muscles of the legs are pointing in two directions, which weakens the push or brace in either direction. Furthermore, it splits intention, which totally reduces the ability to close distance, and weakens grounding.

The reason they did this is because they wanted the back stance to feel more powerful. Turning the back stance into half a horse taps into he weight = work = energy formula, so it does feel more powerful, but it becomes anchored.

They should have concentrated on the horse stance for grounding, and the back stance for closing distance.

The secret is to make it a squat favoring the back leg, the front foot pointed forward, and the back leg almost forward.

My instructor turned both feet forward in his back stance, but he was light and whippy and favored closing distance over grounding.

But, he could ground like a mofo, so he was proving that if you adapt your stance to a specific purpose it becomes MUCH more functional.

The right tool for the right job, you know.

Figure on left has feet turned outward, which gives feeling of power, but the power is 'anchored' to the ground.

Figure on right doesn't have the look or feel of power, but is crouched for maximum forward movement, which is appropriate to the stance.

One doesn't need to look or feel powerful in stance. Power is only needed when you strike or block. To show power before you move can let the opponent know what you are doing.

Chapter Thirteen
Aligning the Feet

When you create your stance you want to align the feet with the rest of the body, and with the purpose you intend for the stance.

Turn the feet forward for charging, analyze the turn of the foot, the arch, the ball and heel, the structure of the ankle, and the rest of the leg upward, for what you are going to do.

If you need extra stop after charging forward in a front stance you might want to explore turning the front foot inward.

If you are summoning more energy you might want to momentarily sink your stance. This is the tip of what I call 'supercharging,' which is when you stomp the foot to aid the focus and energy production (in the tan tien) of a technique.

If you just want to brace a front foot in a front stance so it can't be swept, you might keep it straight and drive weight into the leg.

If you are not moving, but turning tightly, you may want to turn the toes in (or out), as in Pa Kua Chang, which is specifically designed for tight, turning movements.

I would suggest making a list of potential motions, stomping, turning, stepping, pivoting, kicking, etc., for the foot. This starts the logical matrixing of the subject.

And, you will want to make sure that the feet line up with the body. Don't turn the body sideways, and forget to turn the foot with it, for example.

The danger here is that by turning the foot, or setting it up otherwise, you show your intention to an opponent. But there are ways around this. Doing it quickly at the last moment, using it to make the opponent read you wrong, and so on.

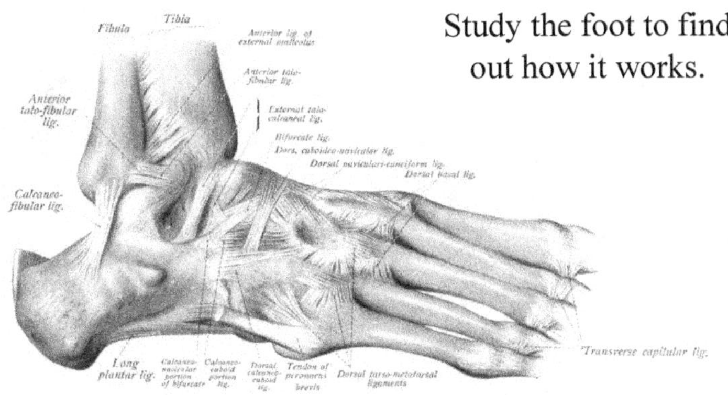

Study the foot to find out how it works.

Chapter Fouteen
Summing Up the Feet and Stances

Sometimes people get lost with all the words and explanation. Thus, it is important to summarize and emphasize what, exactly, you should be doing with the feet and stances.

Two purposes, sinking the weight or launching the weight.
Align the feet with the ground, the rest of your body, and your purpose.
Coil the leg, or legs, making it (them) into a spring.
The Energy Formula is: 'Weight = work = energy.'
Never, even when moving, lose your connection with the earth.

The most important thing to remember is that the stance is not some mystical thing. It is a functional thing and easily defined if you follow the points I have listed here.

If confused, remember this:
Squat. Don't 'strike a stance,' for that very description limits motion.
Squat, and choose whether to be immoveable, or to use the squat for the launching of the body.

The Two Purposes of the Legs!

Sinking the Weight!

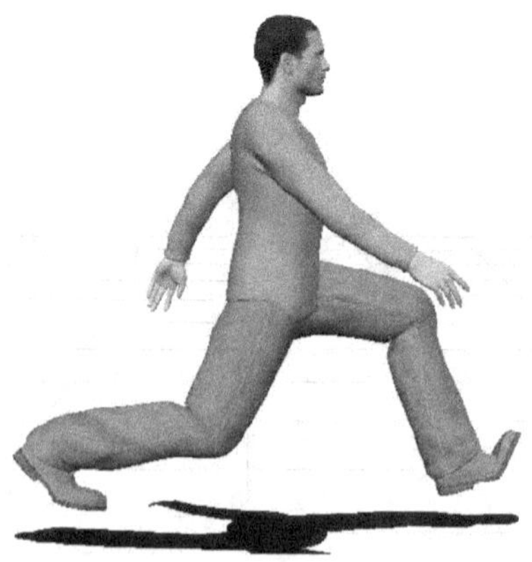

Launching the weight!

Chapter Fifteen
Repetitions

People have a confused idea of the value of repetition in the martial arts. They tend to think of repetition in terms of weightlifting, where you do a certain number of reps, the muscle breaks down, and so on.

The martial arts grow muscle, but by the way.

The real function of training in the martial arts is to train spirit. To grow spirit. To understand the universe.

Think about it this way. A fellow walks to work. It's twenty miles, and then he has to work all day, then he has to walk back.

Maybe a bit of an extreme example, but useful, when you consider how much an army must march.

So how much do you use your muscles when you work out?

Not, 'Oh, I've done a few reps, time to rest.'

But, I must swing the sword until I can do it all day.

I must do not ten kicks, but a thousand kicks…for a warm up.

How do you make your body do this?

Go through the tiredness, and keep going.

And, here's my little secret, and it has to do with kicks.

I initially trained in a class setting. We would do sets of ten kicks. Ten front snaps, ten side thrusts, ten wheels (snap kick on the side with the ball of the foot), ten whatevers.

After I achieved black belt I realized that my kicks were not all I wanted them to be, so I started doing sets of 250 kicks. Front, side, wheel, etc.

Then after some 20 years - I know, I'm a little slow - I realized that my kicks weren't what I wanted. They required effort, I got tired, I wasn't snappy and flexible.

Or maybe I was just getting old.

So I started doing kicks Tai Chi style. I would do them slow, taking the idea of weight out of the kicks, making them light and whippy in my mind.

Intention is superior to the body; get the intention and the body will follow along.

The funny thing is that the more I took the idea of weight out of my kicks, the more powerful they became.

People are sometimes amazed when they see my basic front snap kick. It is faster than a punch, and I'm near 70 years old.

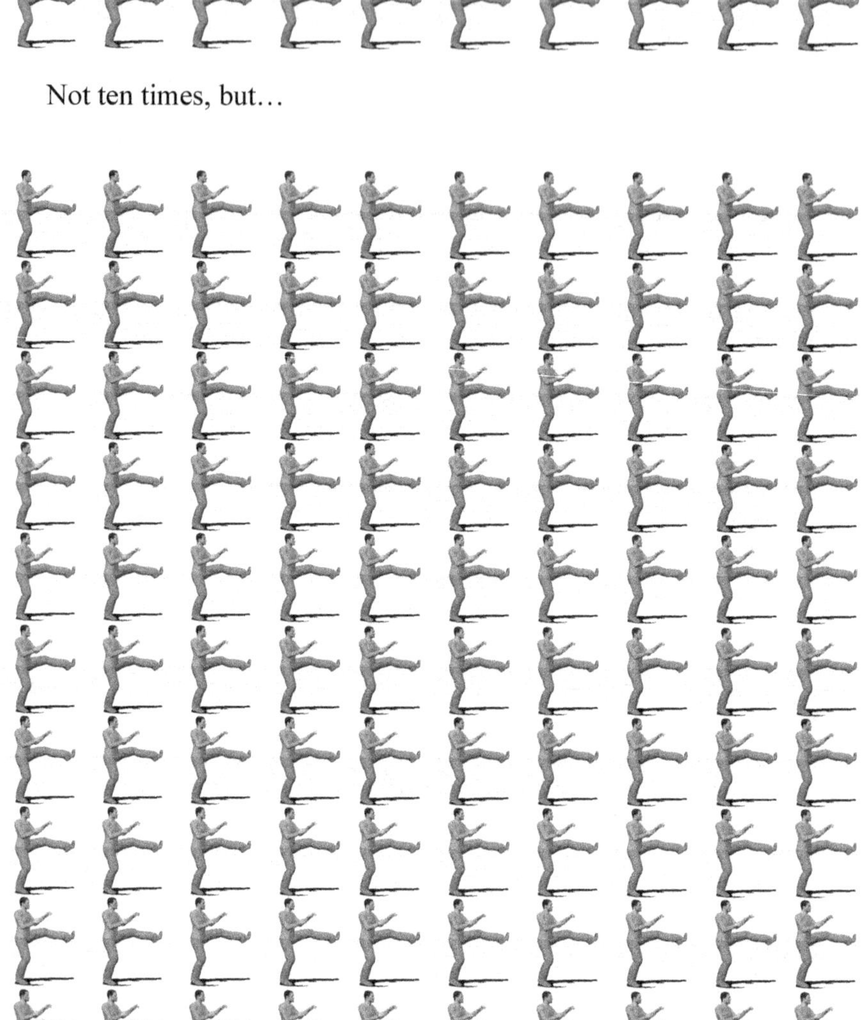

Not ten times, but…

Ten Times Ten!

And times ten again.

Chapter Sixteen
Aligning the Hips

It's always amazing to see some student karate step into a front stance and do a reverse punch, and have butt wiggle.

It's like there's no connect between the person and the purpose of a punch, which is to deliver weight into a strike.

The way to cure this, and a lot of other problems, is to align the hips with what you are doing.

First, the hips should be slightly tucked. This strengthens the back.

Second, if you are punching with the front hand the hips should be turned into the action, aligning with the line of the feet...and the shoulders.

If you are punching with the reverse hand, the hips should be squared. Not over turned, especially in the shoulders, as so many people do, but squared. It is easy to test the function here, simply push or pull on the punch. The energy should be directed down one of the legs and into the ground.

Pull on the punch and the energy goes down the front leg.

Push on the punch and the energy goes down the back leg.

The Japanese say the hips are the cornerstone of the body, and they are right.

The hips are the foundation for the tan tien.

The hips should be low and level.

One way to do this is to assume a front stance and reverse punch. Then pivot into a front stance in the other direction, the other leg, and reverse punch.

Learn how to snap the hips...and without ANY excess butt wiggle.

Check yourself by holding a broom stick across your hips.

When you can do this exercise easily, and the ends of the stick don't wiggle, you have it.

Figure out how to apply this theory to the hips in all stances.

Pivot, slamming the hips hard. If the ends of the stick don't waggle you are doing it right. Apply to other techniques.

Chapter Seventeen
The Purpose of a Punch

I've mentioned this before, and it is time to go into it in depth.

The purpose of a punch is not to 'hit harder.'

Furthermore, you don't need lots of big, massive muscles to have an effective punch.

The purpose of a punch is to transmit weight to another body. So much weight that the other body can't support it and flies away or somehow breaks.

This is true for kicks and blocks, too.

Now, mass sometimes translates as weight, but I find that density of muscle is more important in the martial arts.

You don't want big muscle, you want lean but heavy muscle.

You want the weight of density, and the speed that less mass brings.

The most important thing, however, is not all the stuff I've just told you, because intention is superior to the body, and strong punches can be developed by any shape, any mass, any density set of muscles.

The most important thing is to learn how fragile the universe is.

The universe is, essentially, empty. There's a lot of space in those molecules and atoms.

But we look at a wall and we think it is unbreakable, and the thinking stops our doing.

But if you simply relax, achieve a little 'emptiness' (no distractions…pure intention) in our punching, then the unbreakable becomes breakable.

This actually leads to a rare practice that is legend, but not done by many. The Iron Fist. Or palm, or whatever.

If you pound on a makiwara with your fists too much they become cut and bruised.

So you drop your palm, or the backside of your hand, on a pad. You do this forever and not bruise or cut.

Don't hit…just drop. Let the weight fall without restriction.

What happens is that in the relaxation the emptiness of you begins to appreciate the emptiness of the universe.

At first it doesn't seem to work, but after a few months, if you should have the unfortunate experience of having to slap somebody, or hit, you will be amazed at the breakage you can achieve.

Emptiness is the secret of the universe.

**Striking is the act of transferring more weight
than the target can support.**

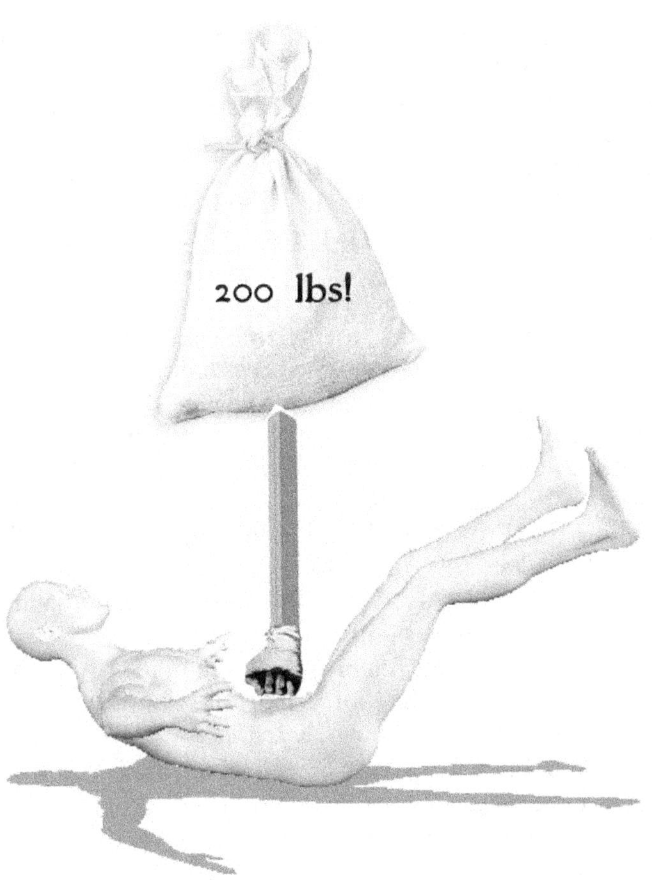

Don't unnecessarily tighten the muscles when punching,
just commit weight without restriction.

Chapter Eighteen
The Mad Monkey Punch

One of the things that people don't consider, when training in the martial arts, is that the martial artist has to be loose, become rigid, be loose, become rigid, and so on, many times as fast as he can.

A fight is not all rigid,; effective striking depends on being loose between he strikes.

One of my favorite training tricks for this is 'The Mad Monkey Punch.' So named after a chop sockey from 1979.

Position the hand, fingers pointed forward, one inch from a bag (wall, pad, whatever).

WITHOUT PULLING THE HAND BACK) go forward and strikes with the fingertips. Then, without drawing back, strike with the second set of knuckles (half fist). Then, without drawing back, strike with the fist.

Repeat. Stay loose in-between strikes.

This prepares you for the short strike. Why a short strike? Because a long strike is too easy to see coming.

And because if you are in a fight you should learn to deliver weight in the shortest distance - and distance is time - possible. Without drawing back. Just go forward in the shortest distance.

Place your fingers on a board. Only go forward and close the hand into a fist. Breaking a board in that manner is one of the simple martial arts tricks.

Over the years I played with the Mad Monkey Punch, and came up with an interesting variation.

Strike with the third finger tip, then the index fingertip, then the third finger first knuckle (third 'half fist' knuckle), the the index finger half knuckle, then the whole fist, pause…another fist.

I would put this to a congo beat, a 'cha cha,' if you will.

Bing, bing, bing bing..bam…bam!

I found the musical overtone, the beat, helped me lose myself in the moment.

I always made sure not to do the drill with impact, or undue stress to the knuckle.

But I kept doing it.

When you see me do those short strokes on a training video, and my partner suddenly grunts with pain, it was the Mad Monkey that helped me along.

The Mad Monkey Punch!

Strike with the fingers,
Don't withdraw.

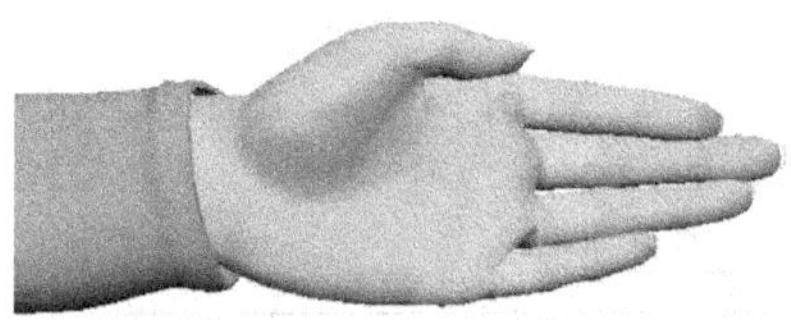

Strike with the half fist,
Don't withdraw.

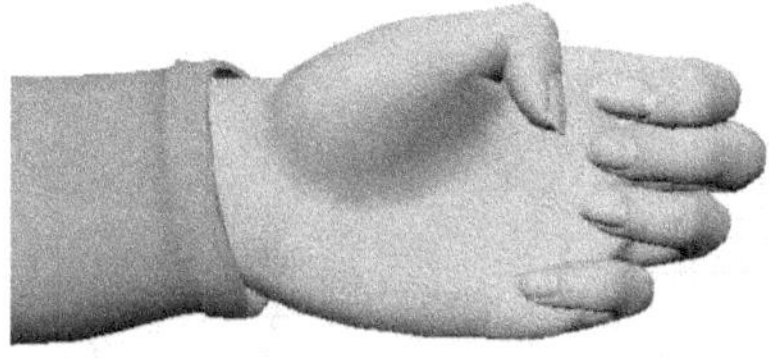

Strike with the fist,
Don't withdraw.

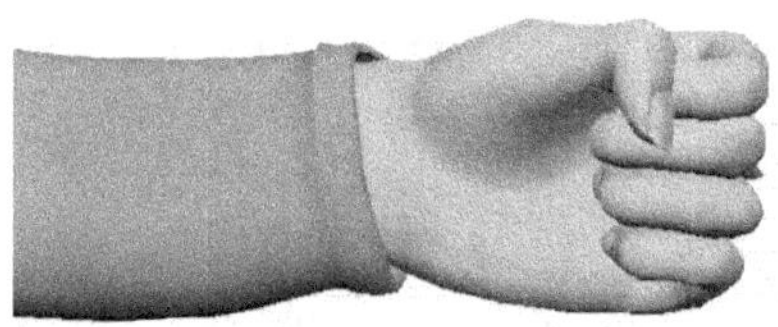

Chapter Nineteen
Loose-Tight

In the Kang Duk Won we would do 'loose-tight:' be loose, make the body rigid at the point of impact (strike or block), then loosen up again.

The beginners would make the whole body rigid, and this is where many of the classical karate styles are stuck. They make the body rigid, and never think about the loose.

The body will run out of energy, but it will never run out of emptiness (loose). So if you see somebody who fights in this manner, by being rigid all the time, hit him a moment or two after he focuses, his body is coming down from being rigid, and it will be more receptive to a nicely delivered strike.

The advanced student would tighten only the fist, or the foot, or whatever body part was being struck.

They would try to tighten only when necessary, and then tighten only the body part being used.

This was difficult not because it was hard, but because people are so unused to using awareness.

Heck, most people don't even understand what awareness is.

Awareness is when you look. And, awareness is when you look inside the body so hard that energy moves to where you look.

Look at your finger, energy is in your finger.

Look at your elbow, energy is in your elbow.

I would always do a sequence before going to sleep: I would be aware inside my finger, then my next finger, and so on, and then through my toes. I feel this helped me be strong, and immune too many illnesses, throughout my life.

Moving along, the expert student would not tighten, but merely have correct body alignment. To strike with the stick of the bones of the arm perfectly aligned.

And not to just strike, but to insert into the other body.

Incidentally, a result of this practice of loose-tight, and of focusing on moving energy by moving awareness, a few of the instructors could take full power kicks to the groin.

Not because they were tough, but because they practiced loose-tight so much it started to move energy around inside their bodies.

It happens naturally, no need for specialized training. At least, it happens naturally for a system that practices loose-tight, and in the proper context of matrixed forms and techniques and assorted training drills.

White is energy;
black is emptiness.

There is energy in the emptiness;
there is emptiness in the power.

A person who learns only energy,
or only emptiness,
Possesses but half an art.

At the end of energy is emptiness;
At the end of emptiness is energy.

A good martial artist lets the energy become empty;
A good martial artist lets the empty become power.

A good martial artist lets power and emptiness co-exist
according to these rules.

Chapter Twenty
Two Kinds of Punches

There are two kinds of punches: the curve and the straight.

Most people train in curved punches, hooks and so on, because boxing has infected the martial arts. Boxing, just so you know, while incredibly efficient, is a sport, one tries to beat his fellow man. Karate is an art, one tries to subdue himself (base desires, etc.)

The karate man usually doesn't train in curved punches enough; he should be able to adapt his art to the different trajectory of the curve.

The boxer doesn't know how to launch the straight punch. He hooks too much, which tends to destroy his connection with the ground.

Good boxers know how to keep the connection, and even in spite of bouncing. Bad boxers don't.

There are two kinds of punches: the snap and the thrust.

Hooked punches thrust, but usually with only shoulder weight.

Straight punches can snap or thrust.

A thrust punch leaves 50% of its weight in the target (opponent's body). The other 50% goes back up the arm.

A snap punch leaves closer to 100% of the weight in the target. The contact is so fleeting the energy doesn't have time to go back up the arm.

A hook punch, though a thrust because of commitment, acts like a snap, leaving much weight. Unfortunately, because of gloves, boxers often never learn how to target the momentary contact. They can't always glance the strike off a target and cause damage; they are stuck in 'must impact.' Thus, there is a contradiction of principles in the hook. A smart boxer will understand the difference in striking with and without the glove.

Incidentally, Karate does have a hooked punch, but most people don't understand how to use it. This is a weakness of training methods, probably because karate was adapted for children and concealed by secret pact of Okinawan masters.

That said, a chop is a wonderful hook. A chop to the neck cuts the connection between computer and support system (mind and body) with much efficiency.

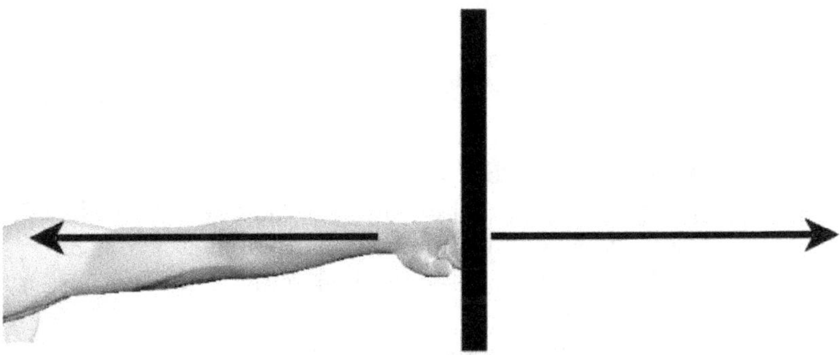

A thrust is heavy and goes through…

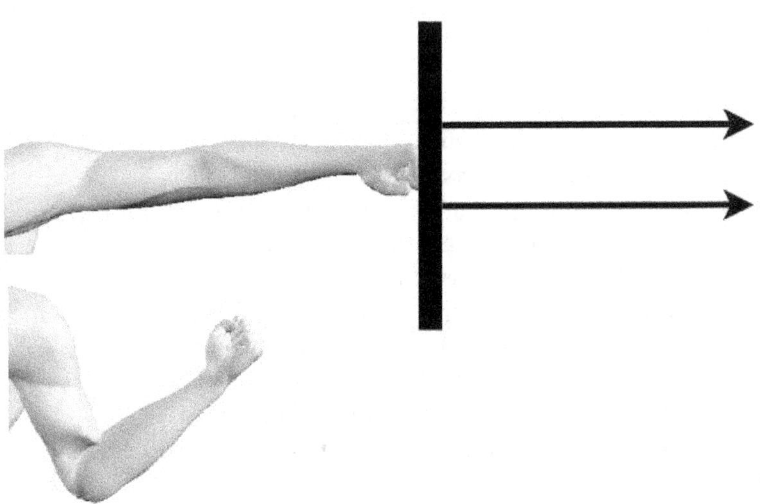

A snap is light but retracts and leaves more energy.

Chapter Twenty-One
Finding the Balanced Posture

Balance is an interesting thing, it is normally halfway between two extremes.

In the matter of a middle block, or ready position.

The arm is stretched, or held against the body. Hold it halfway between stretched and against the body and you have balance.

Hold it halfway between a high block and a low block and it is in the middle of the body.

Hold it not left nor right, and it is between the two.

Relax, so it is squarely in the room.

Don't give it away as a lever, don't allow it to be pushed against the body.

Relax, but don't go limp. Don't relax, but don't be rigid.

But all of this is just the outline of the mind. It's what is in the intention that is important and has to be balanced.

Not unconscious, not overly aware in one direction or the other.

The best exercise I know for teaching this balance is 'Slap Hands.'

Face a partner at handshake distance.

Stand squarely in the room.

Partner A holds his hands together in front of him, pointing at Partner B's mid section, not stretched, not back.

Partner B puts his hands at his sides. He waits.

He waits and watches the eyes, waiting for a blink, a moment of unawareness, a momentary lapse of consciousness.

When it comes, he slaps the hands with one hand.

Partner A brings his hands up to avoid the slap.

Do this every day, and within a month you will be as aware as a Buddha.

Look at the eyes and you will know the person, and you will know him as he knows himself.

Still your flinches until you observe without lapse.

Relax without ever going limp and you will always be ready.

It is a simple matter to translate this simple exercise into punches and blocks.

Soon you will know what the other person is going to do before he does it.

Slap Hands

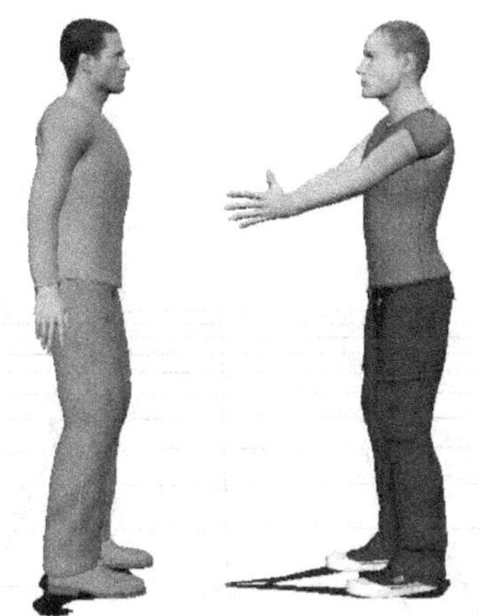

Stand at handshake distance and be still.

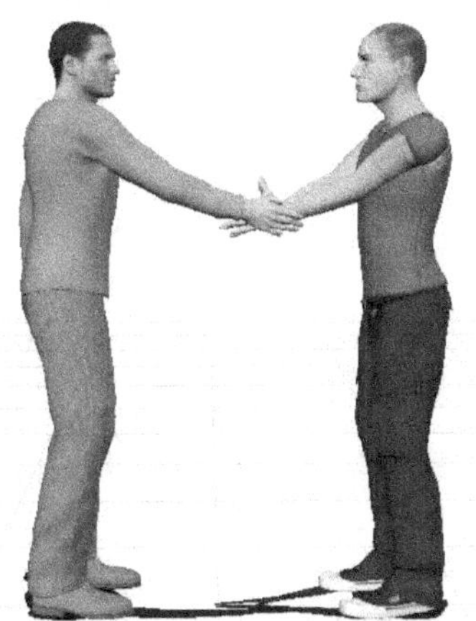

Without flinching, twitching, telegraphing in any manner physical emotional or spiritual, grab his hand.

The partner should attempt to bring his hands back to his shoulders to avoid the grab.

Do not 'over slap,' merely slap to the hand position, not past it.

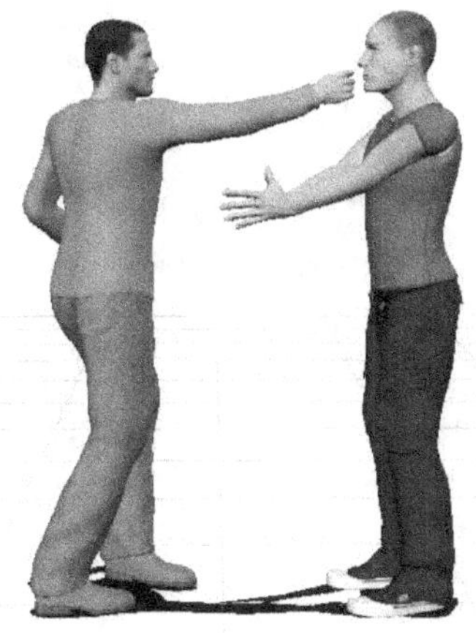

This can be translated easily into a punch, or even a punch and block exercise.

Chapter Twenty-Two
The Knife Hand

Many classical Karateka do the knife hand block with an extended elbow. This is wrong in that it gives the opponent a lever, and it doesn't translate as a block, and it isn't even a good strike.

Done the way these karateka do it, this block sums up all that is worthless about the classical.

Or, they do it with the elbow too bent, a straight, bobbing up and down move, with the hand pointed up.

Or they do it some other way, but nothing having to do with function.

The right way to do the knife hand block is to circle it up by the ear, cupping the ear, and then circling it down at a slant.

It occupies the same position as a middle block, with the hand is configured and angled to chop.

Done as a chop it can break bones, and offer a spear tip for counter.

The Knife Hand Block

Figure on left has arm over extended, it becomes a lever, is not balanced (as described in earlier chapter on balancing).

Figure on right is correct. Block is balanced, energy is aligned down the arm to the tan tien.

Chapter Twenty-Three
The High Block

Most martial artists train the classical so that the high block just raises up. There isn't much attention, or the attention given is wrong, concerning how the arm is slanted, how far from the head it should be, and so on.

The correct way to do it is to bring it up like an uppercut, then pop the elbow outward. The arm should be slanted, a loose fist above the forehead (this angle gives the most resistance in the most effortless manner), like a roof about to deflect rain.

The High Block

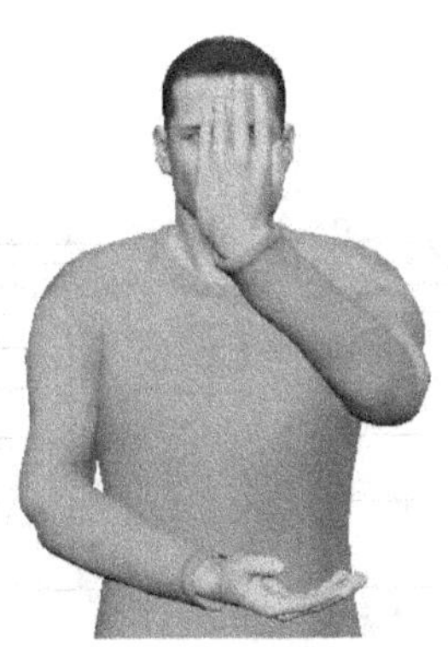

Bring the hand up the center line. It should be loose.
As it passes the face pop the elbow outward into the position as you become momentarily tight.

Chapter Twenty-Four
Come from the Center

One of the things I never hear any more is that the martial art arts must be based on the center.

That is, they must be constructed from the tan tien.

Outgoing motion must follow certain arcs to completion, and result in very sound mechanical structure of the body.

The uppercut that starts the high block must go up the center line of the body, then build a triangle over the head.

When doing the inward middle block the arm must explode from the tan tien, twisting and cutting across an incoming punch.

This holds true for kicks. All kicks must create arc or line that leads back to the tan tien. It is up to the student to have his knee high enough, to create a perfection of arc that translates into the real world, is beautiful even as it is powerful and deadly.

This holds true even for the structure of the stances; they must create triangles with the tan tien at the top and the feet providing the base.

Triangles, arcs and structures all must adhere to certain mechanical principles.

Sometimes people complain that the martial arts are in two pieces, there is freestyle, and then there are the classical forms.

This shouldn't be, but is because people don't understand the mechanical structure that is the body, and how to use the principles in the chaos of actual combat.

To come from the center breath down to the tan tien, let the energy go from the tan tien out the limbs.

Everything must occur with CBM (Coordinated Body Motion), each part of the body moving in accord with every other part of the body.

Even the three principles of power: thrusting, rotating and grounding, must follow these rules. Each type of power analyzed in accord to the move it is being used in. All three types of power must be coordinated until they act as one, which will, incidentally, result in that mystical thing called 'chi power.'

Chapter Twenty-Five
The Two Triangles

The body is comprised of triangles.

There are two major triangles.

The lower triangle has as its three points the feet and the tan tien.

The upper triangle has as its three points the shoulders and the tan tien.

There are minor triangles all throughout the body.

There is the minor triangle who points are the hand, the elbow and the shoulder, or the hip, the knee and the foot.

You can extend the upper triangle to be hand to to hand to tan tien.

There are many ways to configure the body, but adherence to the triangles, and the proper angles within the triangles, make the body able to resist without being stiff. Utilize 'body testing' to improve these angles and the body's abilities.

An item to be noted is that the less you move the tan tien the more efficient your art.

This means that when you kick, for instance, you don't lean backwards with the shoulders. The upper triangle should stay balanced on top of the lower triangle.

When you move you want the tan tien to take the shortest, straightest line. This means you are moving your weight the least amount, but for the most impact.

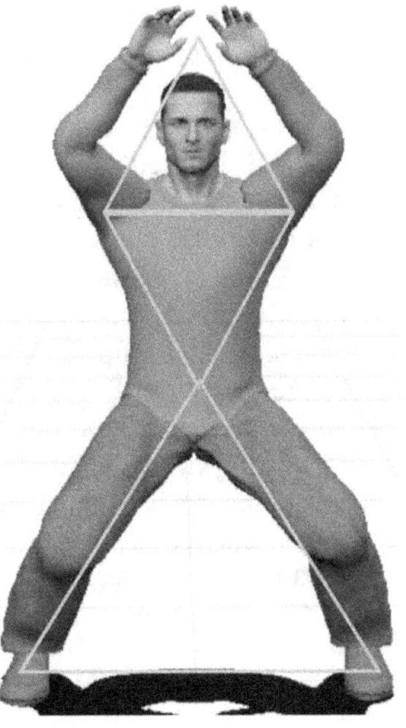

You could, of course, assign the body different geometric shapes. You can make squares out of the horse stance, or across the hips and the shoulders. You can create arcs and circles out of motion. And so on.

But the base of it all is the triangle. The lower triangle, because of its base, is the most stable geometric shape for stances, and there improves your whole art.

And the point involving the tan tien in the upper triangle helps conceptualize breathing and relaxing.

Chapter Twenty-Six
Supercharging

The essence of grounding is to sink the weight. To connect to the ground. To connect the body to the ground.

In stances one postures like a cat, low to the ground, ready to pounce, yet unable to be moved.

When striking or blocking one must connect the motor of the body to the earth so that the machine of the body can function properly.

Machines don't work if they aren't fastened down. They spin and tilt and fall over. Let alone waste energy.

The body is no different.

When kicking one should sink the weight.

If you straighten the support leg when kicking you risk detaching the machine of the body from the earth.

If you sink as you kick then the Energy formula kicks in.

Weight = Work = Energy

One exercise we used to do in the Kang Duk Won was to deliver a push kick to the waist (belt) of the partner. The partner would grab the leg as if he had caught the kick.

We would give a little hop, and push the leg out, essentially delivering another kick, at the same time the weight went down the leg into the floor.

We learned to be stable, not to have our kicks caught, and how to get out of having our kicks caught.

We also learned something I refer to as 'supercharging.'

Supercharging is when you strike at the moment of dropping the weight, and specifically stomping the foot.

Stomping the foot while striking increases the weight up the leg, feeds more energy into the tan tien, and creates more power for a technique.

Chapter Twenty-Seven
The Side Kick

The side kick is a fundamental kick. It is meat and potatoes; it gets the job done.

If people do it right.

First, bring the leg up and thrust it out. It must not swing up from the ground, for it will literally graze the target. Instead, lift it up and drive it like a nail.

Second, turn the support foot about 135 degrees away from the direction of the kick. This will turn the hips into the kick, which will commit the weight of the body. No foot, no hips, no weight, no kick.

Third, sink the weight. Bend the support foot and drive weight into the ground. This will increase the weight, which increases the work, which increases the energy.

Fourth, NEVER do a knife edge with the foot. If you try to walk on the edge of your foot it will hurt, this proves that the foot configuration isn't up to the load bearing impact in a powerful side kick. Instead, stomp with the heel, or the whole bottom of the foot.

Sink the weight.

Bend the support knee.

Kick with the flat of the foot (heel).

Bring the knee up and align with target before kicking.

Turn the support foot slightly away.

Turn the hips into the action.

Breath out (kiai) with impact!

Chapter Twenty-Eight
The Parts of the Foot

You can kick with four parts of the foot.

The heel. Good for stomping and side kicking.

The ball of the foot. Good for snap kick and wheel kick.

The instep. Good for roundhouse (same as wheel kick, but for the different part of the foot you are using.

The toes.

Many years ago I was in the army. I met a fellow from Chicago who knew karate, this was back in the seventies when nobody knew karate, and we began friends and worked out together.

When the company had to do self defense drills we would stay in the back row, take a step backward, and practice forms and freestyle.

The drill instructors, realizing that we were light years ahead of their training, didn't say a word.

One night I was in the head (the bathroom), and he walked in.

He said, 'Watch this.'

He kicked the partition for the toilet with his toes. Straight toes. Like a spear hand, but with his bare foot.

Sure, he could use the other parts of the foot, but his school specialized in toe kicks.

The partition, thick plywood, bent way in and snapped back. He wasn't far from breaking that sucker.

I tell that story to encourage people to specialize in kicks. Not to just do them because the class is doing them, but to find a training method and work through distraction and the idea of pain, to focus their awareness until they can do such things as this.

Karate isn't for supermen, but it can make supermen. It just takes dedication, practice, persistence, and a certain fanaticism.

Ball of foot.

Heel.

Instep.

Toes.

Chapter Twenty-Nine
The Wheel Kick

The wheel kick is a powerful weapon, when correctly done. It is especially useful for tournament fighting.

First, it is a front snap kick on the side.

Second, bring the leg to the chamber position, sideways from the hip and close to the body.

Third, don't pause in the chamber position, the kick must be like a whip, liquid from ground to target, and from target to ground.

Fourth, sink the weight (bend the support foot) when kicking.

Fifth, make sure you turn the support foot about 135 degrees away from the line to the target.

I should probably define the difference between the wheel and the round kick here.

To make best use of the instep the roundhouse swings in more from the side.

The wheel, using the ball of the foot, comes from a slightly different angle, driving in with more of a slam of the hips.

The difference can be summed up like this: the roundhouse is like a baseball bat. The wheel is like a ball peen hammer.

Either kick can be used, you should be comfortable with either, and know that they can require slightly different situations.

I once asked my instructor which kick he preferred. (I knew better than to ask him which was better.)

He said, 'There's more art in the wheel kick.'

It took me a while to figure that out, then I agreed with him.

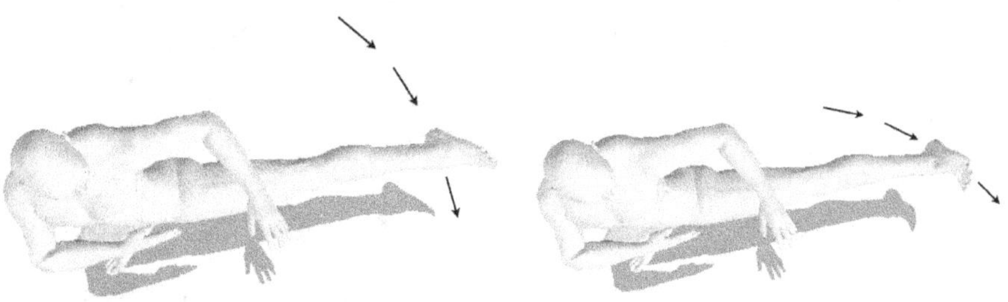

Roundhouse uses the instep
And comes in more from the side.

Wheel uses the ball of the foot
and comes in at a sharper angle.

Chapter Thirty
On Kicking Through

I watch the MMA, and I shudder at the kicks.

They often don't seem to think about the configuration of the foot, which part of the foot they are hitting with. Worse, they swing through, turning their back on the other person.

It is a bad idea to turn your back, you are exposing targets and taking weapons out of the action.

If a guy punches and spins through it is easy to step in and strike. All you have to watch out for is the spinning back fist.

If a guy kick and spins through, likewise, you can rush in and launch attacks before he is set.

I am always surprised that people don't do this in tournaments, let alone MMA fights.

But people are busy dancing, they don't understand how to move while keeping a ground, and so they are not in a position to launch their bodies forward.

And, if a person turns his back for a spinning backlist or spinning foot of some kind, I am almost shocked by how people let them get away with it.

Again, too much bouncing, not enough set and ready to go.

The stances are simply not being set up properly, and not being used.

People kick through, they don't retract, all you need to do is lean back, slap the foot past, then rush in and punch the kidney, or push them over.

Chapter Thirty-One
The Martial Arts as Calisthenics

I always chuckle, somewhat sadly, when somebody tells me they have to get in shape before they learn karate.

At one point, I am told, the Japanese were conscripting Okinawans. Every once in a while, amongst the scrawny peasants, a muscular brute would appear.

He studied Karate.

The most efficient body shaping/strength building exercise in the world is body calisthenics.

In three months the US army (or other American military) takes nutritionally deficient saps and changes them into tall standing, muscular soldiers who can march till noon, fight a battle, and march home.

Now let's talk about the martial arts as calisthenics.

Every time you do a front stance you are doing a type of lunge.

Every time you do a horse stance you are doing a type of squat.

Every time you bend the legs into any stance you are doing incredibly efficient muscle building exercises. Exercises that result not just in strength, but in flexibility and durability.

Every time you snap the muscles in a block or punch you are tightening muscles, getting rid of fat and building lean.

Every time you move you are using muscles.

Every time you strike a bag, or a body, you are entering 'resistance' training.

And somebody wants to 'get in shape' before he does a class where he…gets in shape.

And the muscle you build lasts well into old age.

And, just for clarification, warm ups are not about building strength. They are for loosening up, getting a touch more flexible, getting the body ready to do the more rigorous exercises that are karate.

The deeper your horse the better your squat.

Chapter Thirty-Two
Basic-Basics

Fellows who have made it to Black Belt, legitimate Black Belts, usually do what I am about to tell you. But I never hear them, or their instructors, give instruction the how and the why for what they are doing. I call these things the Basic-Basics.

RELAX ~ Try to relax every moment of your life. Even when punching and kicking, try to relax utterly and completely around the moments of focused energy. Really good martial artists can even relax while punching and kicking.

GROUND ~ Sink your weight. Connect yourself to the ground. Actually imagine, until you can serious feel, an energy connection with the ground. Attend to the Energy Formula:

Weight = Work = Energy

BREATH ~ Breath to the tan tien (the one point), which is an energy center located a couple of inches below the belly button. No, oxygen won't travel below the lungs, but breathing to the bottom of the lungs creates a wave of energy that travels down to the tan tien. When you breath to the tan tien you should be able to feel your outstretched finger tips tingle.
Further, breath out when the body expands, and in when the body contracts.
Further, breath out when you strike, kick or block. Breath (as if) into the body part doing the striking, or being struck.

ALIGN THE BODY ~ Make sure the body is correctly aligned, that the parts of the body, from foot to fist, are in the proper order for the most efficient ability to resist weight.

CBM (COORDINATED BODY MOTION) ~ Make sure you move all parts of the body at the same time. Start everything at the same time, stop everything at the same time. All parts of the body must support the same intention.

Past these advices, concentrate on the principles of your art. Do you flow? Focus? some other principle? Strive to understand and implement those principles.

Chapter Thirty-Three
Monkey in a Box

I do the Monkey in a Box drill for every class. It builds strength and flexibility in the ground position. It builds muscles through out the body, makes the joints flexible, can be used to train the student to roll, handle himself on the ground, and return to the fighting position.

Drill is done with the hands and feet being the corners of a square.

First, the right foot goes under and the left arm goes over.

Then the left foot goes under and the right arm goes over. And so on.

It's easy to figure out how to roll into the box, out of the box, add kicks, etc.

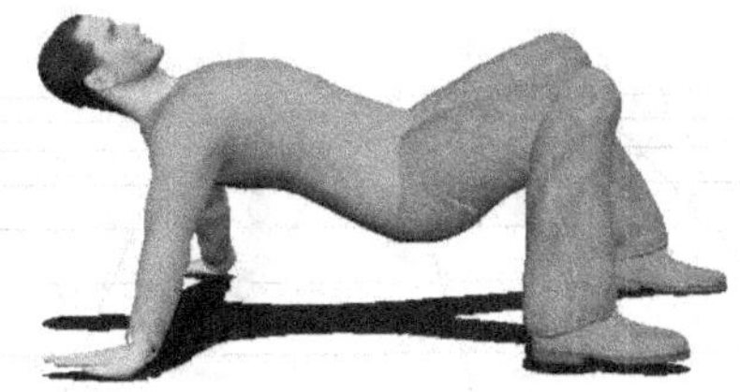

Chapter Thirty-Four
Belly Push Ups

I am always surprised at how little people understand what is happening when you hit, or get hit.

When you strike somebody you are trying to put weight onto their frame so that the frame collapses, or is in some way rendered unfunctional.

When you get hit you are trying to resist incoming weight.

Obviously, letting people hit you, as in practicing the techniques, will train you to handle this rapid increase of weight to your body (part).

But there need to be exercises that will help train the body, will specifically strengthen the body and train it to this concept of getting struck.   I usually have my students do Belly Push Ups.

Have one student lay on the ground on his back.

Have the other student put his fists on the first student's belly and do push ups.

This is what it feels like, or at least it duplicates in slow motion, when somebody strikes you in the belly.

So one student strengthens his arms for punching (being able to resist the sudden explosion of weight through the arms that results when striking), and the other student strengthens the belly muscles so as to be able to resist the sudden increase of weight that results from being struck in the belly.

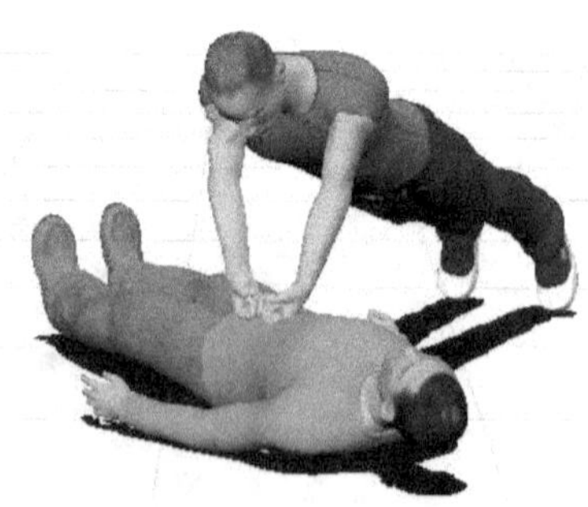

Chapter Thirty-Five
Straight Finger Push Ups

I have already told you of my instructor, who could thrust his finger through a board (it was thin plywood) and leave a hole.

So what type of exercises did he do to get there?

First, he did the forms.

He worked on the basic-basics until the outer world no longer distracted him.

And he did finger tip push ups.

First, on the hands.

Then on the backs of the hands.

Then on the knuckles (fists).

Then on the half fist knuckles.

Then on the fingers.

Then on the thumbs.

Then on two fingers.

Then one finger.

One finger each hand, the finger totally straight. A straight line from the tip of the finger through the hand, up the arms to the shoulders.

What most people don't realize is that there are no muscles in the hands. The muscles that activate the fingers are in the forearms.

So by doing push ups on single fingers one has to have strong forearms, but more important, he has to understand that this is all a matter of balance.

You have to balance the muscles in the forearms so they don't quiver, so they can hold the finger straight.

It is not that the fingers quiver while doing this, it is that the forearms can't hold them steady.

Mind you, this will usually take some years to go through the hands,
fist, knuckles and finally reach straight
 fingers, but this is the highest level of
art.

It is the highest level of body
control, and the highest level of
technique, and it doesn't come from
strength, it comes from just being
aware enough to balance the muscles
in your forearms enough so that they
can keep the fingers straight.

Chapter Thirty-Six
Distance

What most people don't know is that time is a measurement of distance.

Sure, you can measure distance with a ruler, but how long does it take to cover that distance?

That's where time comes in, and that's where it becomes incredibly important in the martial arts.

Timing is a knowledge of how before a punch hits you, and can you sneak in before time arrives.

There are six ranges: weapons, kicking, punching, kneeing, elbowing, and weapons. You should train so that they are capable at all distances, and can shift distance if the other person happens to be more capable,.

Actually, while I encourage a thorough understanding of the six ranges, the six distances really break down into three distances.

You enter a fight, close the distance, and end the fight.

You can actually do this at any range. You could enter the fight with a kick, closing the distance with a leg, and knocking out with that same kick. All in one.

You can do this with any weapon.

Most fights, however, are not so clean cut in their analysis.

So one should practice closing the distance by using the feet, transitioning to the hands, transitioning to the knees, transitioning to the elbows, and finally locking and taking down.

In a perfect world you would be launching knock outs with each weapon, but it is not a perfect world.

What will likely happen is that strikes will miss, be deflected, and positions will shift and warp so that you can never quite line up the sequence of kick, punch, knee, elbow and grapple.

That's okay.

Train so kicks can transition to punches, knees, elbows, and grappling.

Then train so that punches can transition to kicks, knees, elbows, and grappling.

And so on through all the ranges.

Train so that if any range in a sequence is negated you can slide right through to another weapon.

Remember this:

Control the distance and you control the fight!

TIME IS DISTANCE!

Distance is merely the word for the concept that means 'how long will it take my fist to reach his chin.'

If you can understand this - that time is distance - it unlocks the martial arts, which is nothing more than measuring the distance (time) it takes to reach a target, a position, an ideal situation.

Chapter Thirty-Seven
Muscle Versus Energy

The body has many systems.

There is the skeletal, the lymphatic, the nervous, the muscular, and so on.

What most people don't know, at all, except in the most odd and arcane mystical theories of 'chi,' is that the body has energy.

When you use muscle you send a message (an impulse) to the nerves, you tell the muscles to contract or let loose, and you move.

Well, it is actually much more complicated than that, but that will do for a likable simplicity.

What people don't know is that energy is easier to use, requires less effort.

The problem is that they think that energy is a thin, little filament that runs through the body and you have to meditate on the meridians and all that.

No, no no.

Your whole body is a conduit. Energy builds in your torso and flows through your limbs.

When you stand in a stance, sink your weight and breath, you should be able to feel energy going down your legs and grabbing the ground like magnets. When you do this you should feel a sensation from the viewpoint of your legs, it should feel like you are in your legs. When you do this your connection CANNOT be broken.

You should be able to use your arms in like manner. If you grab somebody it should be like you have closed a circle of energy in your hands, and the other person CANNOT break the grip.

When you strike somebody it should feel like a vast weight is minutely moved, and they fly away from you.

You can hold people on the ground with a mere finger.

You can touch them anywhere, and they will twitch and fall like rag dolls struck with a two by four.

And, here is the funny thing, the more you use muscle, the less you will be able to use energy.

The less you use muscle, the more you will be able to use energy.

Energy likes a vacuum of effort, and responds to the lightest of thoughts.

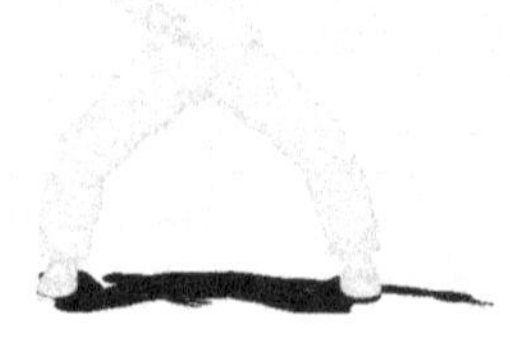

Chapter Thirty-Eight
Muscle v Dynamic Tension v Chi

Body calisthenics are the best exercise for the body. Using the body weight will not detract from CBM, even if you focus on a small group of exercises and neglect certain parts of your body.

I'm not a big fan of weight lifting as so many people abuse it, and the result is UBM (Uncoordinated Bpdy Motion).

Dynamic Tension, the playing of one muscle against another, is not bad. It is still in the realm of body calisthenics.

Solo Dynamic tension (I don't know what else to call it) is when you tighten one muscle through a range of motion.

This could be a short motion, as in a punch, or it could be an series of motions, such as holding a teacup on saucer and moving it in a figure eight position.

This seems to be fairly unique to Karate (martial arts), and effects the body on a long lasting, deep level. I sometimes wonder if it is effecting the body on a cellular level.

I do know that the simple act of tightening the fist a few hundred times, manically, in the course of a work out, makes the limbs dense and strong.

But here's the funny thing, if you want to build chi power, do the motions without the muscle, without the effort, and focus on feeling energy run through the body.

You can run energy through meridians, though that tends to be another type of practice.

But you can run energy as if it is a vast commodity.

Use your imagination and feel it slosh inside your body like water in a bath tub. Feel it course down your arms and legs like water in a fireman's hose.

Swirl it, pump it, extend it outside your body.

Learn how to do tricks.

Chapter Thirty-Nine
Align Applications

You must align the applications of your art.

If you use karate style blocks, your whole art must be devoted to understanding karate style blocks. If you are studying a throwing art, your art must be devoted to the throws, and never putting a karate style block in to it.

I know so many people will rail at this, may not even finish this page, but the logic is sound here: DON'T CROSS CONCEPTS!

For example, don't put a parry in to a karate style art. Even if you find one in the form, or it looks neat when somebody does it, or is even more efficient.

The reasoning is that you must keep each art pure.

I remember learning kenpo. Learned the first two forms, and then I had to learn, I think it was in the applications, a 'windshield wiper' block. I don't know the real name, but it was a quick motion, sliding the hand back towards the face and deflecting an incoming strike.

It's a good block, but it went against kenpo techniques, and it made the art harder to learn. It 'crossed' concepts, without taking any concepts to a complete understanding.

It was heady. learning all the concepts, but I watched people get confused and drop out.

And it is no wonder people spend lifetimes in the art, marveling at its depth. What they are actually doing is continuously unraveling that which cannot be unraveled, lost in a trap, gaining huge ability, but never mastering the art.

Jack of all trades, master of none.

I once asked a fellow, he owned a school up in Northern California, if he wanted to learn matrixing.

He misunderstood, thought matrixing was an art. He declined, saying there was still so much in his art that he had to figure out.

And he was delighted to be lost in such a vast puzzle.

But he could have understood his art, and started picking up whole arts and understanding them, and in a fraction of the time.

Then his abilities would have been awesome.

But as it was, stuck in his art, he was good, but would never be great.

When you learn each art in this smaller format, and truly understand each art conceptually, then, in the end, they will naturally merge, with no planning or forethought.

To solve the martial arts one need merely define a logical method for each situation represented in this graph.

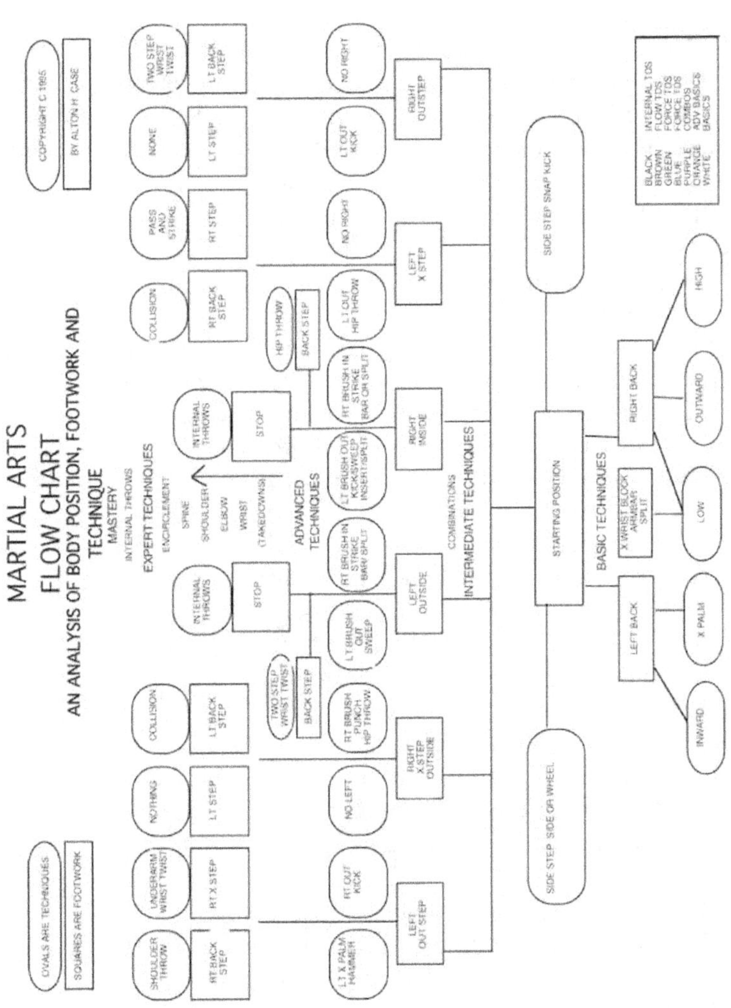

Chapter Forty
Make Concepts Progressive.

One of my big breakthroughs was when I realized how the concepts of the martial arts aligned, how they actually progressed.

First is block and counter. Basic karate. Makes Karate one of the best first arts one can study.

The problem, of course, is that people don't know what to do after they get the block and counter (or whatever basic concept your art is providing), so they go crazy mixing concepts, putting advanced with basic, never considering how confusing this is to the students.

Second is block and counter with the same hand.

Third is block and counter simultaneously. You do them both at the same time.

Fourth is simply counter. See what they are going to do before they do it, and strike first.

The problem is that martial arts get so mixed up that logic fails, therefore the pathway to intuition is gone, and the student never arrives at the end of the game. Which is to say he never achieves those mystical abilities of legend, but just keeps muddling along, not realizing that the pathway has been all mixed up, the signposts changed, the rules skewed.

Past the sequence of block and counter from karate one goes into other concepts.

These concepts are usually based on flow. Going with, instead of stopping the attack. Guiding and manipulating.

Wing Chun traps the hands.

Preying Mantis guides the hands.

Tai Chi guides the whole body.

Aikido guides the whole body while in motion.

But all of these arts have confused the basics, left the simplicity of karate, and have not provided for an easy ascent into mastery.

And it is easy.

Line up the concepts, make them progressive, teach them in order, and you will be shocked at how fast you learn, and how easily all the arts merge into one.

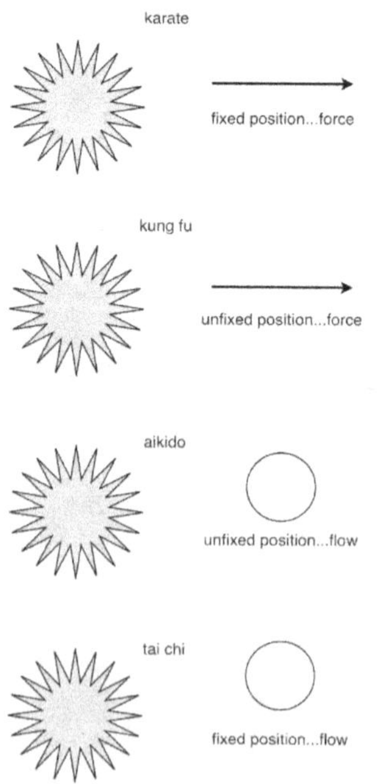

Chapter Forty-One
Align the Body

There are two sides to this idea.

One, align the body from the fist to the ground.

You can check this by pressing on the fist, block, body part in question, whatever.

If the body gives way, or even feels we—if it can't resist without effort—then you need to check your alignment.

CBM, to get ahead of myself here, is nothing more than the alignment of the body in motion.

Two, you need to analyze the body so that the feet align with knees align with the hips align with the shoulder align with the elbows align with the wrists.

This can get confusing.

For instance, if you assume a front stance and strike with the rear hand (reverse punch), then your hips need to be 'squared' to the opponent.

If you are punching with the lead hand (lunging punch), then you need to have the hips on the same line as the feet and shoulders.

It is shocking how many people don't understand this, but you can see, when they punch, that there hips merely occupy a place in space. They don't turn in the right direction so as to align with the rest of the body.

And, of course, it isn't just the hips.

People hold the shoulder too far back, or extend them too far, which destroys the line of them in relation to (they should be directly above) the hips, the feet,
and so on.

This is why we have forms, so that we can go through the forms, examine a variety of postures and how to make the change from one posture to another.

Chapter Forty-Two
Analyze Each Joint for Function

This is a simple one.

Is the elbow a ball and socket? Or a hinge?

How about the hips?

The neck?

Or is the neck a combination of factors?

And, here's an interesting one: analyze the muscles just below and above the joint being considered.

What muscles make the joint contract?

What muscles make a joint expand?

And what part of the muscles is working at what angle of the joint?

Is there an optimal angle at which the muscles work best? (Easiest…with the least effort.)

When you move the joint does energy run through the muscle?

Feel the muscles, physically, with your hands, and analyze how the muscle contracts.

Now, when you do the forms (from which all techniques derive), analyze your motion so that you use muscles purely.

Don't twist as you push with the leg, for while the hips might be built to rotate (ball and socket), they don't respond well when the pressure increases. This is because the muscles doing the pushing are in the calf, and the push depends not on the ball and socket of the hip, but the hinge of the knee.

Now do this for all your joints.

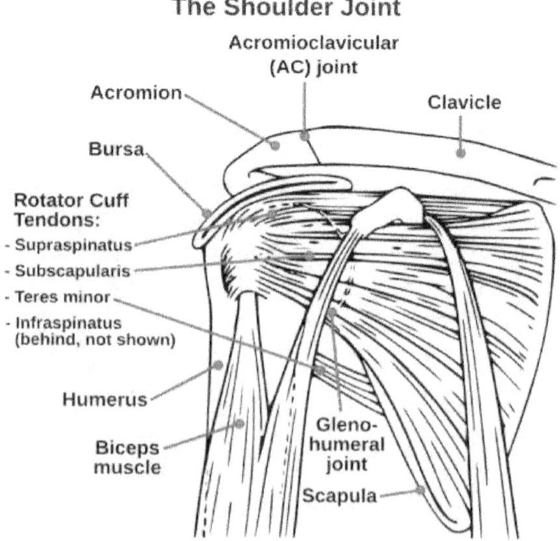

Chapter Forty-Three
Analyze the Dichotomy of the Limbs

The universe is dichotomous. That means there are two sides to everything. Good and evil. Left and right. Man and woman.

What's interesting is that this concept trickles down to the smallest things. Take, for instance, the leg.

The leg has muscles in the front and back. Thigh and ham.

Tighten one and the leg folds. Tighten the other, and the leg unfolds.

Here's the interesting thing: take a crane stance, stand on one leg, and, in the beginning, the muscles will quiver, the front and back fighting for balance.

This is the secret of yoga, and especially Tai Chi Chuan. In many postures; once the quiver stops balance is attained.

The trick is to move so that there is never a shiver or quiver. Not when you lift, step, shift, or do anything.

Isolate the muscles. Be aware of the muscles on both sides. Move into stance without any back and forth between the muscles and you have balance.

This is a most excellent thing to do, as you will not render the body into parts, but rather find an interesting level of CBM.

Chapter Forty-Four
Analyze Direction part one

There are six directions.

I use the six directions, incidentally, when I analyze motion logically;   when I matrix.

The six directions are:

up

down

left

right

forward

backward

There is a punch. I decide which direction I will use to handle the incoming force. Do I block up, down, left, right, forward, or backward?

Then, the block having been executed, I analyze which direction I will use for the counter: do I move my arm up, down, left, right, forward, backward?

I do not ignore body motion in this solution. Taking into account everything: which side he has forward, which weapon does he favor, is he on a suspicious surface, is the light shining through a window, is there a dog in the room, are friends (his or mine) coming, is there a weapon laying on the table, what is his emotion, what clothes he is wearing, what did he eat that morning, and so on.

And, surprisingly, when it all kicks in you do actually become aware of all that stuff. You become aware of everything. Makes fighting a heady experience of enlightenment, else people wouldn't have been fighting for all their lifetimes in all the universes.

And, all the data absorbed, a decision is reached and I finally move.

The human being being what he is…it only took a nano second.

In fact, zen to be believed, it happened between the seconds of time.

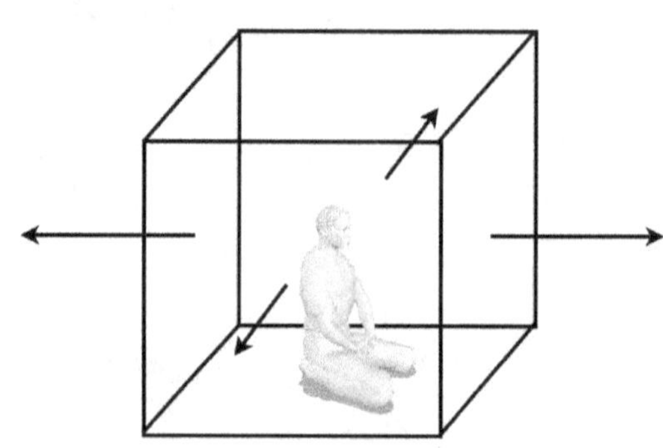

Chapter Forty-Five
Analyze Direction part two

To reverse engineer a bit; to go back to where I began analyzing motion.

During World War One the American flying ace was Eddie Rickenbacker.

Eddie had the most aerial kills, was a race car driver and designer, and was a pioneer in aviation, piloting Eastern Airlines for many years.

For me, Eddie had a precise message.

He would visualize himself at the center of a moving sphere, then visualize attacks coming into that sphere from any direction and speed. He would then solve the problem of the attack in his head.

And this is how he became America's greatest flying ace.

I took this lesson to heart and analyzed the martial arts.

Interestingly, there are several theories, or constructs, provided by a variety of arts.

Do you use the four doors and eight gates of Wing Chun?

Do you use the up down, side to side theory of karate?

Do you use the eight directions of Pa Kua Chang?

And, to complicate matters…do you use the standing absorption of Tai Chi, or the moving acceptance of Aikido?

And so on.

My solution was to pose problems in each of these arts, and solve them according to art, and then to put them all together so see where there was overlap, contradiction, and so on.

Now it is your problem.

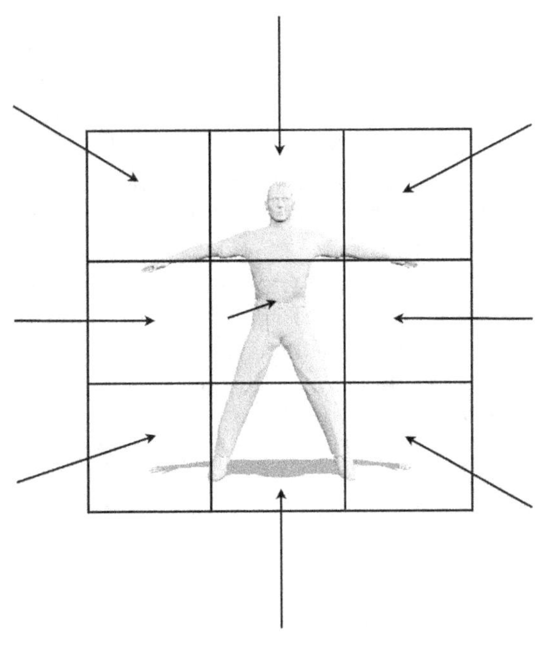

Chapter Forty-Six
Analyze Motion and Emotion

I'm quite proud of the fact that I am the sole discoverer of a unique fact concerning humanity.

Emotion.

Everybody talks about emotion, experiences emotion, but doesn't understand what emotion actually is.

This is because emotion is a layer, a barrier, we project to protect ourselves.

And, it is a communication device, unfortunately largely ignored.

And, it manifests, especially in matters of conflict/combat, when a person is being overwhelmed, or wants to overwhelm.

But nobody knows what it is! Nobody has defined it past a form of energy that emanates from the body (mind) during times of stress or significance.

So I am proud (not in an arrogant sense, for that would be an emotion) that I figured this oddity out.

Too speak precisely: Emotion is nothing more than motion inside the head.

Conflicts happen, the mind absorbs this conflict, mirrors this conflict, and begins generating the 'static' that is wavelength to precise emotions. It is generating a solution of mental energy. Rightly or wrongly.

Thus, when one analyzes direction of combat one has to analyze the complication of the direction of emotion.

What is going on inside the opponent's head?

Is he emotionally running? No matter what physical direction he is taking? Is he in fear even while attacking?

Is he emotionally coming at you? No matter what physical direction he is taking? Is he angry even while retreating?

This offers a magnificent opportunity for matrixing.

If you truly want to reach a high level of art you need to look at each motion in connection with each emotion.

A punch with fear, anger, bravery, cowardice, etc.

A takedown with terror, heroism, conservatism, high aesthetics, and so on.

Motion $\longleftrightarrow$ **Emotion**

Chapter Forty-Seven
Analyze Geometry

There are only three shapes, but these are the shapes of the universe.

The three shapes are the circle, the triangle, and the square.

Everything in the universe is constructed of these three shapes.

A house is square, a doorknob is round.

To find an interstellar distance one uses triangles.

The body, in the martial arts, is comprised of these three shapes.

The feet to the tan tien describe a triangle.

Motion is generally an arc, except when it is a straight line, which is created by an arc of muscle.

The hips and the shoulders describe a square, and there are particular waprings of this square when one does punches and blocks.

A spiral is a circle being stretched out. Many forms of energy are actually spiraletic in nature.

A donut is a torus, which is a circle in a circle.

You can track the motion of a planet by establishing two triangles, then using those triangulated points to make a square. This is the essence of algebra.

Mathematics, the root of all sciences, is nothing more than a system made up by man to measure the universe.

This science must be applied to stances, the configuration of strikes and blocks, and all the motion a human body is capable of imagining.

What is truly interesting is that man thinks with shapes, and there are only three shapes. So the very thought of mankind manifests in geometry.

All attacks and defenses, all interchanges between human bodies, any bodies, can be described and understood in terms of geometry.

The unfortunate fact is that many people will scoff at the idea of knowing mathematics being important to analyzing the martial arts.

The world is full of fools.

Everything in the universe is
constructed of...
Triangles
Squares
Circles

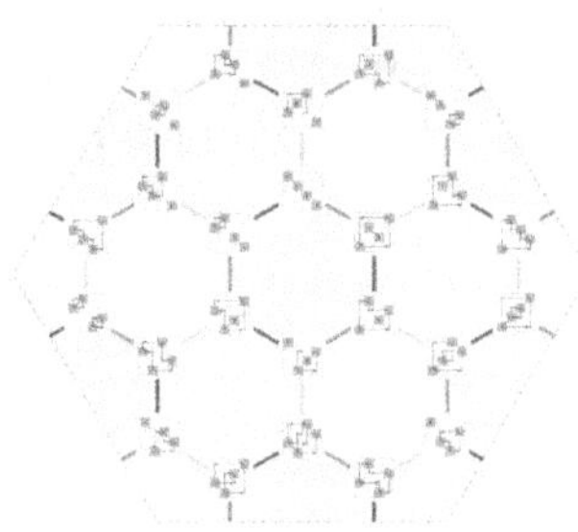

Chapter Forty-Eight
The Force/Flow Formula

This is the truth:

For something to be true the opposite must also be true.

This describes the universe…in ALL its dichotomy.

There are many extrapolations of this truth, especially in the martial arts. The following Force/Flow formula is the first rule of the martial arts.

If the force is greater flow it,
if the flow is greater force it.

Unfortunately,   the universe being a universe of force, most martial arts are built around force. If the force is greater force it. If the force is lesser, force it.

This short-sightedness is amazing in that people adhering to it will follow this advice to their demise.

Even intelligent martial arts, advertising their systems as 'hard/soft,' have no clue as to the real meaning of this concept.

The only systems approaching this truth are tai chi and aikido, but these systems tend to go too soft, claiming flow as a solution. If the force is greater flow it, if the force is lesser flow it. Which is just the other side of a very warped coin.

If one really wants to get to the truth of the force/flow formula they need to matrix it.

If the force/flow is greater…force/flow it.
If the force/flow is greater…flow/force it.
If the flow/force is greater…flow/force it.
If the flow/force is greater…force/flow it.

Now go through all the techniques of the martial arts and apply these four potentials to every single one.

Now you have the truth of the martial arts, and of the universe.

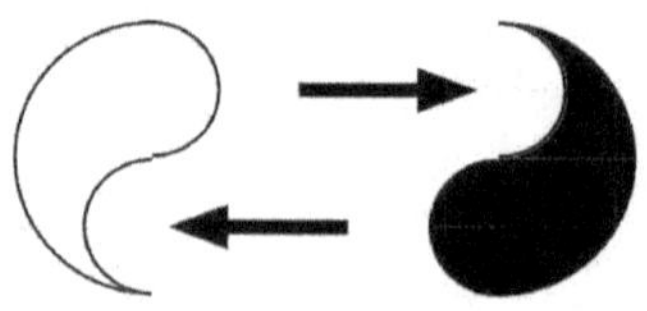

Chapter Forty-Nine
The Use of Weapons

To learn how to use weapons one does not have to study a specific weapon under a specific master for a number of years.

If one is learning a classical system, one just picks up whatever weapon he wants to learn and plugs it into the form.

Do Heian Two (Pinan Two) from classical karate while holding a knife in one hand.

Do the techniques, looking for workability.

Toss out what doesn't work, fix what does work in your mind through LOTS of practice.

Now do the form, and techniques, with two knife.

Do the form, and techniques, many times with the knives held in different manners.

Do the form, and techniques, while hold a sword.

Two swords.

A sword and a knife.

A club and a knife.

How does changing from edged to non-edged change things?

What works and what doesn't work?

A club and a garbage can lid.

A short whip.

And so on.

The thing about weapons is that you can't just pick them up, twirl them a few times and think you know them.

You have to practice them until they are as familiar as a knife and fork and spoon.

You have to practice them until they are extensions of your arms.

Of your very spirit.

And, make sure you shift the forms through force and flow.

Some weapons work best with flow (creating arcs of motion), some work best with force (stopping arcs of motion).

So do your form without focus, moving the hands through circles and arcs without focus, and examine the weapons from those viewpoints.

And don't forget to have an opponent come at you with the weapon(s) you are practicing with.

Chapter Fifty
The Range of Weapons

I have said that he who controls distance controls the fight.

Think about it, if you are punching and the guy moves an inch or two forward or back, it effects the value of the punch. If he even turns a little, the punch can slide off, or even damage your wrist.

So, you have to train to figure out the right weapon for the right distance, and train yourself to stay in the 'now,' so you don't miss.

The weapons break down like this:

Weapons (variety of distances depending on the weapon)

Kick (a variety of kicks create a variety of distances and motions)

Punch (straight or hooked)

Knee (grabbing somebody when you knee stabilizes distance)

Elbow (excellent)

Grab Arts (hard to defend because when somebody closes to grapple they are negating distance)

Each of these distances has shades and deviations galore.

MMA, for instance, only a couple of workable takedowns, but they are really workable. Once on the ground distances are measured in finer and finer tolerances and times.

At any rate, being fond of forms/techniques for training (classical martial arts) I simply plug weapons into techniques.

For instance, a simple high block against a punch, a curved punch, a club, a sword, a gun, a garbage can thrown, etc.

I know it sounds funny, and odd, and maybe even unworkable, but one of the most valuable things one can learn in the martial arts is what doesn't work. Thus, the unworkable can be avoided.

And, in using this simple technique against a variety of weapons, one learns how to make the technique work against everything.

So go through your techniques, work them against knives, guns, clubs, throwing stars, and whatever else comes to mind.

Matrix weapons against techniques and you will REALLY learn the martial arts.

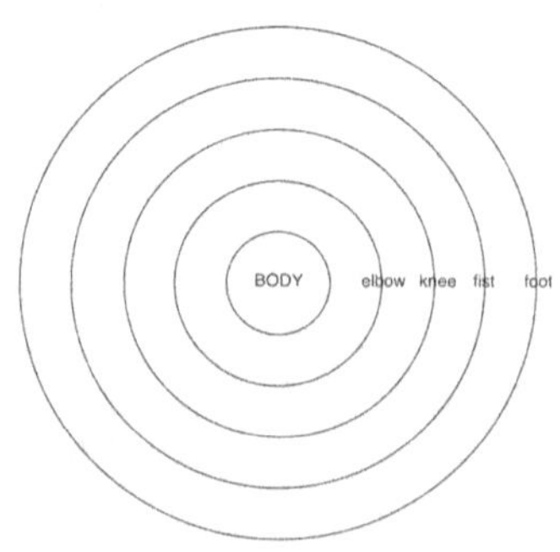

Chapter Fifty-One
The Eight Catchers

It sort of surprising, but there are only eight attacks in the martial arts, which means there need only be eight defenses.

Obviously, this is loose, but think about it: if somebody is holding a sword, they will likely attack with the sword. They aren't going to drop the sword (give up their advantage) and start punching.

The same holds true for knives, guns, clubs, and so on.

So I boiled it down to basic weapons. Yes, you'll have to adapt and deviate and do all sorts of things. But, here are the Eight Catchers.

Sword catcher ~ X wrist high block to arm bar.
Foot catcher ~ hook and lift the leg
Club catcher ~ Two step to wrist twist, split, etc.
Fist catcher ~ Slap/Grab, or art of choice
Thug catcher ~ attack from rear
Knife catcher ~X wrist low block
Spear catcher ~ spinning up the pole
Gun catcher ~ cross slap barrel and wrist

These are pretty efficient and teach one a wide variety of motion.

Thug catcher I teach last, as it requires a certain degree of intuition, which intuition will be gained by practicing the other techniques. Simply have somebody stand, or sit, facing one direction, and slowly chop down at the back of his head. The attacker may have to wait for the defender to move at first, but the training will eventually take hold and the defender will begin moving in time with the attack. The defender needs to forget about the attack to make it work.

Fist catcher I use Slap Grab, but any art, if matrixed, or done long enough, will result in the student becoming intuitive.

I like to teach catchers after a person has a hand to hand system to black belt.

A person with a weapon will be loath to give up the advantage of that weapon.

Chapter Fifty-Two
CBM

CBM stands for Coordinated Body Motion. It is when you move all parts of the body as one unit.

This means starting all the body parts into motion at the same, and stopping all body parts motion at the same time.

It means analyzing muscles, mass, and all aspects of the structure so that each body part contributes to the motion proportionately.

In the past this has been very loosely defined, with the result that many students don't understand, and don't get the benefits they expect. Or, at least, they take forever to become competent and enter into the intuitive side of the martial arts.

The instructions usually consist of some vague generality: 'move the body as one unit.' Which is correct, but totally lacking in instruction, and gives no clear cut idea of what it is you are trying to do and why.

I began doing this because I saw other people doing 'butt wiggle' when they were punching, and realized it was a lack of control, dispersion of power, and very inefficient.

So I began trying to move the foot at exactly the same time as the hand.   Which led to looking at the body, and trying to move the body, hips and all, at the same time.

Which led to analyzing how much each muscle pushed the specific mass of body it was 'tethered' to.

I eliminated hip wiggle, started the process which would lead me to realize that no force is better than lots of force, which led me to analyzing whole arts, and so on.

Mind you, my research was odd, sometimes haphazard, out of order, consisted of mistakes and reverse engineering from those mistakes, and so on.

But the end result is this: You need to coordinate the parts of your body if you ever want to control your body.

And, by the way, it is VERY hard to control somebody else's body if you can't control your own body.

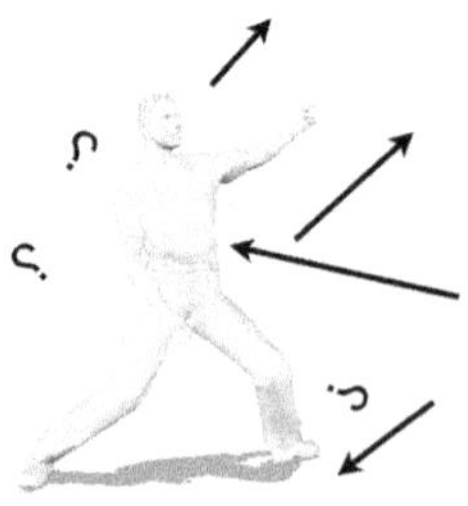

At the least, we are talking about years of extra study that wouldn't be necessary if you just CBMed.

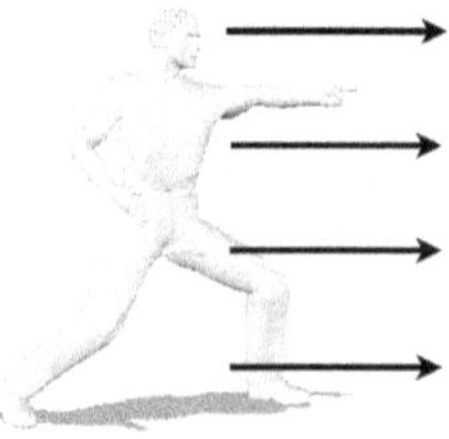

Chapter Fifty-Three
CBMing to Chi Power

People study the martial arts for years and never experience this thing called 'chi power,' which is silly if they understood the depths to which one must CBM their body.

First, you have to CBM all body motion. Moves the hands and feet and torso and so on at the same time. Adjust them so they each contribute appropriately and in the correct percentage.

Second, don't forget to include the Basic-Basics in that CBM.

You have to coordinate relaxing, breathing and sinking. You have to CBM this into the motion of the body. CBMing alignment in motion, is of course, CBMing the body.

Third, and here's the one that leads directly to chi power, and which nobody understands, you must CBM the three elements of power: dropping the weight (grounding), turning the hips (rotation), and thrusting the weight of the body.

Generally, the body will be able to use each of these Basic-Basics in a motion. For instance, one will sink the weight and turn the hips as they thrust forward.

But you have to analyze each technique, each posture and motion, to configure the correct percentage of each of these items.

A lunging punch (stepping forward into a front stance with the right foot as you punch with the right hand) might have 60% thrust, 25% grounding, and 15% hip rotation.

A punch out of the horse stance to the side might have 10% thrusting, 5% hip rotation, and 85% grounding.

So you have to look at the body in motion, and examine how much of each Basic-Basic should be used.

Forms are very handy for this.

In fact, most boxing arts do almost none of this, offering only such generalities as 'throw your weight into that punch,' which tells the student absolutely nothing. It is only years of experience that will remind him of that simple instruction.

How simple it would have been if he had forms, and a good teacher to point out
the simple trick of
how to CBM.

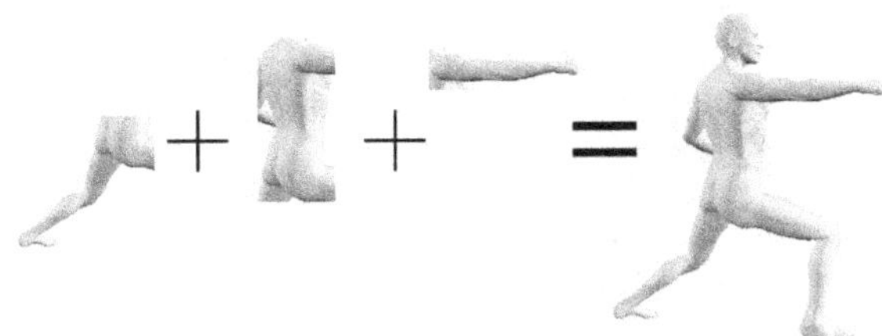

Chapter Fifty-Four
The Universe is a Mirror (part one)

I remember, when I first started the martial arts, reading everything I could. Most mystical of all were the books on zen. But all that reading was good for something, I finally figured something out.

The universe is backwards.

This is easy to understand: you are not the screen upon which the universe is shown, you are the projector, and you make the universe happen.

Thus, they universe reflects what you do, what you think, all the contraptions of You the Spirit.

It responds to thoughts, not to the wishes for fishes and trek of the human mind.

What is not so easy to understand is that because the universe mirrors you, you always perceive it as you would perceive yourself in a mirror, in backwards fashion.

This makes the universe difficult to manipulate.

Unless, of course, you have done enough martial arts to realize yourself as the creator and the universe as the creation, then the universe is easy to perceive, and to make work.

You are terribly strong, a wonder that can create cities and rockets to the stars; and the truth is that while it takes great force to accomplish this, the idea that set it all in motion is soft.

You are a creature of love; the result is that you force yourself into perversions and think it is natural.

Everything in the universe is backwards, and this is proven by the theorem:

For something to be true the opposite must also be true.

This theorem only becomes real as a postulate, however, when you have done enough martial arts to realize your true self; that you are a spirit and the universe is your creation.

For something to be true, the opposite must also be true.

Chapter Fifty-Five
The Universe is a Mirror (part two)

To help yourself understand that the universe is backwards it is helpful to do one thing:

Do your forms backwards.

This is an interesting procedure which is not available to people who study martial arts without forms. Those people do not get the benefit: no boxer has ever realized that the universe is backwards.

If you do your forms beginning with a step to the left and a low block, do your form with a step to the right and a low block. And continue the form, in that reverse fashion, all the way through.

At first your mind will boggle, you will have to think, it will seem counter intuitive.

But can you fight anybody if you are trained only on one side?

Sure, doing the forms will eventually help you achieve the idea that the universe is backwards, but it will take wa-a-ay too long.

Doing this right/left method will cut your time in half.

After all, you do your techniques on both sides, why not the forms from which they come?

And, once you are adept at this, try one more step, cut your time in half again, and do the forms backwards.

If you end the form by stepping to the natural stance from a front stance with a punch, try stepping from the natural stance into the front stand punch, and continue the form in reverse right to the beginning.

Then do the form in reverse on the other side.

And, in the beginning you will probably be doing the blocks and strikes in reverse, try actually following the path of the form in motion. So you don't just do a block, you reverse the arcs of motion to assume a position.

This is really weird, looks a bit like moonwalking, but for a whole form.

The idea here is to become so incredibly facile that you achieve the liquid aspect that is at the heart of all motion.

Chapter Fifty-Six
Matching V Opposing

The interesting thing is that the procedure of the last two chapters manifests in freestyle.

To effectively freestyle one must know what his opponent is doing.

First, he must get a picture, he must duplicate his opponent, in his mind.

Then he must solve the problem presented, and this often involves, because the universe is backwards, and because the picture of the opponent is often backwards in the mind, some interesting mental gymnastics.

But once you know the universe is backwards, and you understand that your mind is turning everything around, AND YOU HAVE PRACTICED YOUR FORMS BACKWARDS AND IN REVERSE…the problem becomes easy to solve.

To sum it up, you must not oppose your opponent, for that keeps everything backwards in your mind.

You must match your opponent, be a mirror, make your actions duplicate his, then shift them slightly, ever so slightly, from his motion into your motion, and thus create a defense.

The easiest way to do this is to practice the forms backwards and reverse, and then hold to a matching stance in your freestyle.

If you have an opposing stance then you have an imperfect mirror.

If you have an opposing stance your mind will more than likely become opposing, and you will be fighting your own problem solving abilities.

So take a matching stance: if he has his right foot forward, then so must you. If he has his arms in a certain position, you should assume that position also.

If you duplicate him, then your mind can duplicate, and you can easily adjust and solve whatever problem (fist or foot or throw) he hands you.

Chapter Fifty-Seven
Be a Glove

One of the things that fighters usually don't understand, but people who have done forms, and especially Tai Chi forms, do, is that you must be a glove to his hand.

Don't fight, absorb.

Don't collide, accept.

The universe is comprised of objects colliding.

Force is the collision. Flow is the trajectory to that collision, and the lines and arcs emanating from that collision.

It takes massive amounts of energy to collide; to choose a path and then deliberately run into something.

It takes minimal energy to step aside, adjust, manipulate.

Of course, force is the result of 'Might is Right.' Flow is the result of 'Right is Might.'

Thus, when somebody kicks at you, the beginner, still learning his basics, will respond with a hard block. That is okay, for beginners.

But the master will not collide, he will not muster force and bash or break something.

Instead, he will shift to the side, adjust his hands, and let the kick settle into his grip. Then, a slight turn of the hips, and a throw of magnificent proportion is achieved.

Remember, don't be two fists running into each other, be a glove for that fist threatening to collide. Let the fingers and hand slip into your grip, and slightly wiggle the fingers of the glove. That is all you have to do.

Yes, you are amazingly strong, but the universe, being backwards, will respond more to the slight thought than the thundering fist; Force doesn't control force, it just destroys it. Only Flow can control force.

Be a glove, let the attacker enter and accept him with your technique.

Chapter Fifty-Eight
The Eyes Have It

One of the biggest problems people have, in the martial arts and life itself, is where to put the eyes.

A lot of instructors tell you to 'unfocus' the eyes on the body, try to see everything.

Some instructors tell you to watch the hands and feet.

My own instructor said to watch the body; he said the eyes could fool you.

The fact is…The eyes are the windows to a man's soul.

Watch the eyes and you can read minds. It may take some practice, a few thousand times through the forms, but you can read minds.

What I ask students is that if they are walking down the street and a car heads for them, should they watch the driver, or the car?

If they watch the car they will get hit. There is no telling what the car will do.

But if they watch the driver they can see what the case is going to do.

The driver is in charge of the car, it is him you have to watch.

In the martial arts you have to see the spirit, you have to see the human being who is directing the body.

The interesting thing is that people who advocate watching hands or feet, or the whole body, are not teaching you to confront the person.

Some people think you shouldn't look people in the eyes, that it is rude, that it might cause a fight, and other things.

The fact is that I have gotten out of nearly every fight that I was offered by simply looking my opponent in the eyes.

If I can see them, they can see me.

If I can divine the spirit's intentions, then the spirit can divine mine.

So I look people in the eyes, no matter how angry or stupid they are, and they see a person who can see them, who isn't afraid, and they always back off.

It's people who are afraid that can't look people in the eyes, so why be like them?

And, on the other hand, if there is a bully, he doesn't want to be seen. He is afraid if you look at him, and, like a cockroach, will scuttle away.

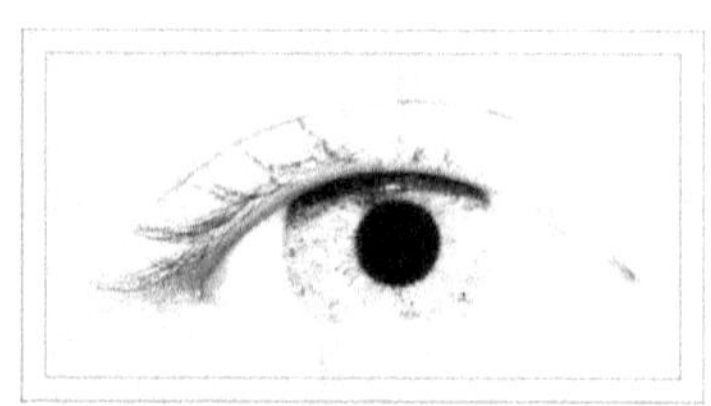

Chapter Fifty-Nine
Wedge the Body

When one practices freestyle one should wedge the body; stand with the body edge on to the opponent, and move to unwedge the opponent's body.

When you stand wedge on you are trying to present as many weapons as you can, and show as few targets as possible.

When you move around an opponent you are trying to manipulate him so that he has as few weapons as possible, and as many targets as possible.

Stand so that it looks like you can kick him with either leg, yet you can still lift the front leg to check an attack, and so that you can attack, retreat, or move to the sides, easily, and without leaning in any direction.

You especially don't want your opponent to detect a lean.

In other words, even in freestyle, stand squarely in the front.

When you move there are several modes you can follow.

Move in and out, never letting him establish a distance, never letting him establish a time in which to attack you.

Or, circle one way or the other, constantly making him shift, never letting him sink his weight and explode towards you. As soon as it looks like he is getting set, you move. As soon as he settles in to the idea that you are circling to the left, go to the right.

Essentially, you should be spiraling in for the attack, keeping your body protected as you expose his.

Move right, or left, so that you have your weapons, and the opponent presents targets.

Chapter Sixty
Create an Alley

When free styling, keep your hands midway between up and down, left and right, to and from.

In other words, take the center four squares of the chess board.

You should actually point your arms at his shoulders. This will make him go in or around. It is an easy task to redirect him if he has already settled for a circuitous path.

The hands should present an alley.

If he enters the alley you simply shift into an inward block, blocking or breaking, closing his body for your counter.

If he goes around the hands you simply open up, exposing his body.

Always seek to be in the most advantageous position. Spiral in on the attack giving him nothing but a choice of whether to enter the alley or go around.

He becomes predictable should you adhere to this strategy.

And, to make him super predictable, and assure your win, open the alley slightly, let him see the opening. When he enters the alley it is Now you know what he will do, and he becomes, as I said, super predictable.

Make an alley with your hands, widen to make attacker come into the alley, close to make him go around. Once he is predictable he is easy to handle.

Chapter Sixty-One
Step on the Distance

As I have said, he who controls the distance controls the fight.

To control distance is the same as controlling time, for time is nothing but a measurement for distance.

One of the best things you can do, in a fight, is step on the other fellow's distance.

There is a perimeter around a person. It usually coincides with the reach of his outstretched hand.

If you shuffle forward and put your foot on this perimeter the other fellow will twitch. This is what I call 'Stepping on Distance.'

There is nothing more fun than stepping on somebody's distance, on the edge of his personal space, watching his energy twitch, and charging in the middle of the twitch.

It is very fun to manipulate where a person will move by stepping on his distance.

Step on his distance without showing any openings and he will back up.

Angle in to the right as you step on his distance, and he will move to his right. Angle in to the left as you step on his distance and he will move to the left.

You can steer a person to the exact spot you want him in before the physical fight ever stops.

You can practice this in groups of people, making subtle moves and watching as people attempt to protect their personal space.

If a person is aware enough not to be guided he is no threat to you, as he is aware, and aware people don't get in fights. Only unaware people are so low as to fight.

Eventually you will get to the point where you can simply shift, not even move, just shift, and people will respond in the way you wish.

Currently I'm working on subtle hand gestures and light thoughts to get people to move the way I want them to.

82

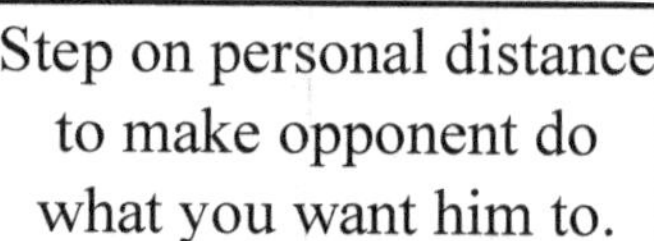

Step on personal distance
to make opponent do
what you want him to.

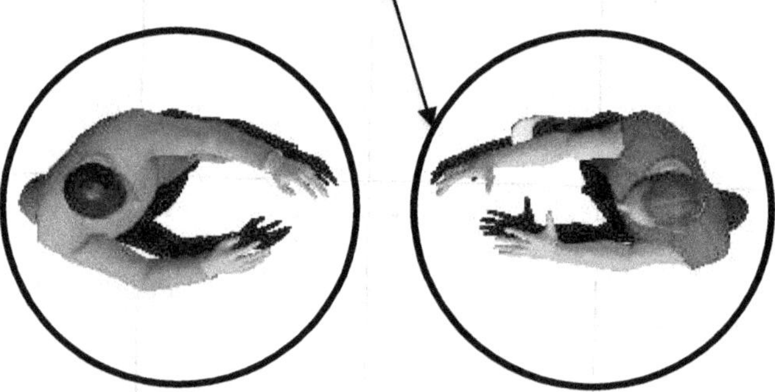

Chapter Sixty-Two
Faking

Faking only works on unaware people.

A person who has become aware won't be fooled; he will respond only to the degree that he should.

If a person punches, he blocks, or moves in whatever appropriate manner he has trained himself to.

If a person throws a half a punch (a fake), he will only do a half a block, then, as the punch stops and retracts, he will likewise stop and retract.

Once you have become advanced in the martial arts fakes become a ridiculous expenditure of energy with no purpose.

He fakes and you punch; who's going to win?

I remember when I first started to understand this. I was studying at the Kang Duk Won, and I was free styling a fellow named Gary. Gary had been studying with Joe Lewis, and he stopped the freestyle and educated me that there were three types of fighters: runners, chargers and blockers.

By making a sudden move towards me he could gauge my response, know which type of fighter I was, then choose his strategy accordingly.

He said I was a blocker. I hadn't backed up, I hadn't charged, I had merely lifted my hands as if to block, so I was a blocker. I would stand my ground and fight.

And I thought how inadequate his strategy was.

I had raised my hands only enough to block because I didn't feel any commitment coming from him. No need to back up. I didn't charge because he hadn't, in his assessing fake, come close enough for me to launch an attack.

You see, I was fighting in the 'now,' and that condition is senior to any assignment of labels.

So don't ignore these labels, go ahead and use them, but keep practicing until you reach the condition of being able to fight in the 'now,' without distraction from past memories or training routines, or from fantasies of strategy formed by the unaware.

TO EXIST IN THE NOW
IS SUPERIOR TO ANY
STRATEGY!

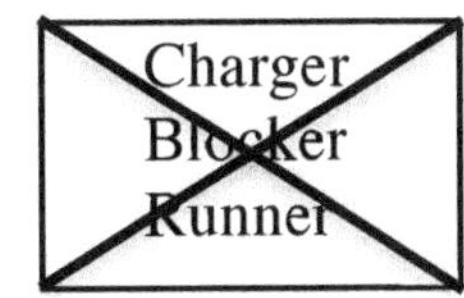

Chapter Sixty-Three
To Grab is to Grab Yourself

I enjoy it when people grab me. After all, if they are using their hand to hold me, they aren't using their hand to strike me. And my hands are now free to strike with.

Any grab can be undone simply by circling your own arm.

If you spiral in as you circle it is even better. You can direct weight into the joint of the opponent grabbing you.

What's really slick is to simply 'pump handle' the opponent's grip.

That is, if he is holding your wrist, drop your hips, which will bend the wrist, and then you can simply thrust your hand towards him and he will be thrown back.

Don't throw the whole body, rather, throw just the joint.

The whole body might weigh a couple of hundred pounds. The wrist weighs a couple of pounds. Once it is bent the flow of energy through it is broken, and it is easy to manipulate.

If you do grab, try not to use the thumb. Rather curl the hand over and guide. Using the thumb sets you up for the opponent to circle, spiral, or bend (the wrist).

Of course, if you decide to dig the thumb into the crown of a bundle of muscle, or a pressure point, or nerve center, or whatever, please do so.

If he grabs you he has immobilized (trapped) one of his arms, and positioned himself predictably.

Chapter Sixty-Four
Grabbing to Attack

One of the things I rarely see in freestyle anymore is the use of the grab.

You set up to strike. You close. You grab his wrist and…side kick, or punch the kidney, or chop the neck.

You pull on the hand while doing this so he can't use it to block.

Pulling unbalances him, straightens him out. While he struggles to attain some sort of equilibrium you pump the kick in, pump that punch in, or twist and drop that chop on the back of his neck.

He will try to pull away, so you have to be ready for that. You must build a good stance.

And, if he chooses to pull, and he is strong, you can actually let him pull you in faster. That's an odd one, but it is real. It just takes a lot of practice.

When I practice I want as much reality as I can get, so I plant my foot on the belt (hip), and push hard.

And, when I punch, I punch the belt semi-hard, and push. That simulates real force, but to an area close to the kidney, but which won't risk damage to your opponent.

And, when I chop to the neck, I turn the hand into a slap and slap the shoulder.

I really have idea why this truly workable trick fell out of practice. We used to do it a lot back in the sixties. Maybe it was just the turn to boxing methods in training.

One of the things that blew my mind was when my instructor grabbed my belt and pulled me in for the kill.

I had thought the belt was sacred, but he just said it was another tool.

Chapter Sixty-Five
Distract to Attack

I always remember the fight I saw in high school.

Two guys were mouthing off, and one of them suddenly shifted his gaze slightly to the side, as if he was looking at somebody behind the other guy, and widened his eyes slightly.

Then, when the other fellow started to turn his head, he let loose with a haymaker that leveled the guy.

Mind you, that punch never would have landed. Too big and wide. But the distraction worked, so it did.

The point is that distractions are EXCELLENT strategy.

The battle starts with a feint by a small group of men to the side, then, when the foe shifts his forces to meet the threat, the real force strikes from another angle.

Excellent. And remember, these are not fakes, but calculated strategies.

So, what kind of feints are there?

Shift your stance so it looks like you have to kick.

Turn your body so it looks like you have to punch with one hand.

Raise your hands as if you are scared, and put them in position for an attack.

Anything and everything.

Throw dirt in the eyes. Spit at him. Yell. Whatever you can do to upset the equilibrium is fine tactics.

That said, I never let people practice feints in fighting practice. You want to train the fellow to respond correctly, so don't mess up the input.

I know that people who fight a lot, do a lot of tournaments, will disagree with this, but they are into fighting, not building a new state of mind, a zen state of mind. You need accurate data, not mind games, to do this.

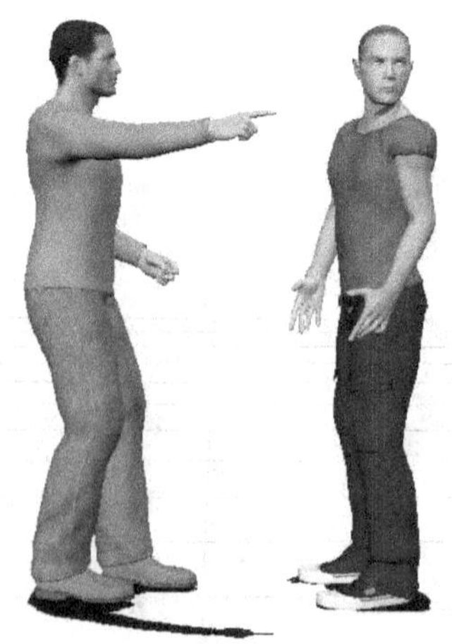

Chapter Sixty-Six
Eliminate Distractions

When you train you are trying to eliminate distractions.

When fighting, you want to distract the other guy, but in your own training, train to never be distracted.

If he motions or spits or fakes, stay focused on what the real attack is.

The martial arts are a discipline in which one trains the mind to shut up.

The mind is a bunch of memories. Shut up the memories and you (the spirit, the fellow in charge of your body and mind) are free to do what you want.

The idea here is that you want to be in one position, then, an attack being perceived, in another position.

You might be standing, then you need to assume a blocking position, or a punching position.

So your feet have to go to the next position in the most efficient manner possible. No fudging or dancing or false steps. Just one position to the next with no distractions.

Same for your hands. From one position, to the next, leaving a line of motion only to enable the body to put weight behind the strike.

Same for the hips, thighs, face, everything.

You are in one position, then the next, with economy of motion, with efficient lines and arcs that only support the one intention being fulfilled.

Where do you practice this?

In the forms.

In the techniques.

Not in freestyle. Freestyle is too random to teach people much about the physics and mechanics of the body.

So practice your forms and techniques with one idea in mind: to get to the next position as efficiently as possible.

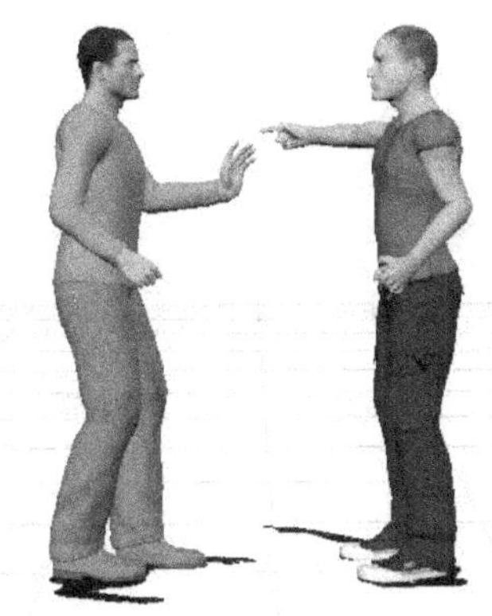

Chapter Sixty-Seven
Don't Twist the Wrist

When you strike somebody with the fist you should not twist the wrist upon impact.

This is contrary to much popular training, wherein the student stands in a horse stance and punches, snapping the fist with a twist of the wrist at the last second.

Punching with a twist of the wrist is done to teach the student how to focus. It is not meant for actual impact.

Assume a push up position on your fists. That is what it feels like when you punch, that weight on the wrist, and it requires a straight wrist.

A straight wrist can support the sudden building of weight when you strike another person.

Now, while you are horizontal and balanced on your fists, try turning the fists.

It is difficult, and, most important, can you feel the deep sense of weakness within the wrist?

The fact is that you need a stable wrist when punching. If you turn the wrist, especially on impact, it de-stabilizes the wrist, and the wrist becomes unable to support the weight involved in striking another body.

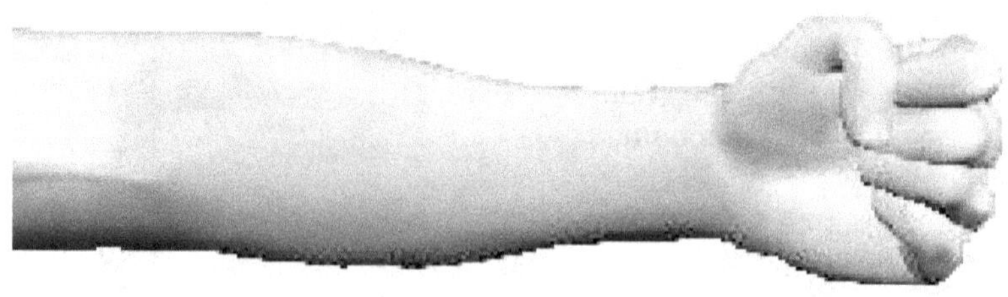

Chapter Sixty-Eight
Making It Work

One of the tragedies that have befallen the martial arts is that somebody is taught a technique, the technique doesn't work, so the student gives it up.

But that technique, if worked on sufficiently, would have become not only workable, but would have elevated the student to new levels of competence.

Way back when I was taught a spin heel kick.

I was taught by somebody who had no business teaching, but I was at the door of black belt and I was absorbing anything and everything I could.

So I practiced the spin heel, turning the body to the rear with the leg outstretched, endlessly.

Never got very good at it, and there was a reason: I didn't believe in the technique. I had enough experience to understand that turning your back on an opponent is risky. Further, When that fellow threw the spin heel i could see it coming a mile away. It was a haymaker, coming all the way in from left field. It might work against the unwary and uneducated, but against me…nah.

BUT, after working on that kick for a couple of years I suddenly realized something. Use the popping motion when you went from a right horse stance to a left horse stance, and try the kick.

Didn't work. Couldn't pop with a swinging kick. The kick couldn't be done fast enough to keep up with the pop of energy from the tan tien.

So I altered the kick, made into a simple side kick.

Suddenly, that thing worked like a charm. I found I could deliver it at punching distance, and so fast that the opponent NEVER figured out what I was doing until it was too late.

In fact, whenever I wanted an easy point, I used that kick.

And nobody else did!

Couldn't't believe it.

The lesson here is that everything can be made to work, but you have to work at it. You have to delve into that technique until you understand why it doesn't work, then adapt it to yourself.

Mind you, I am not saying to waste your time on posers, inefficient techniques wherein the attacker has to wait for you to make the defense.

I'm just telling you to be smart, work hard, and analyze things until you can make them work.

Having Trouble Making a Technique Work?

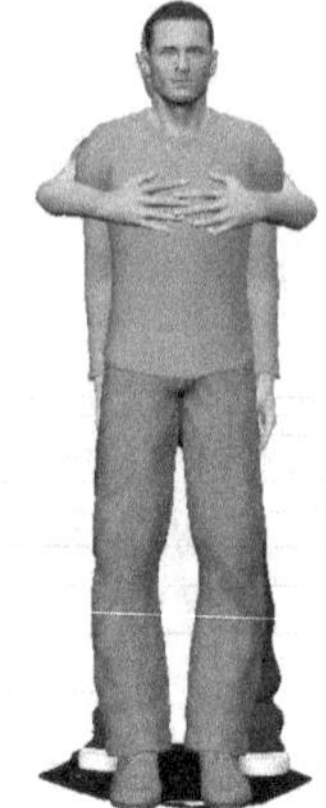

Simply practice it until you can make it work!

Or until you know why it doesn't work!

Chapter Sixty-Nine
The Joy of Combat

The Joy of Combat is probably the single most destructive fact of the martial arts.

The Joy of Combat is the lust for combat, it is the adrenaline addiction that leads to loss of control, broken bones, and a direction away from enlightenment and a better human being.

Simply, one begins fighting and loves it. Something is happening in boring lives, and they become addicted to it.

And it shuts down the path to self discipline. I mean, why do forms when you can fight? Which is like saying: why learn when I can go 'wheee!'

Your purpose in the martial arts should be to seek the higher path, to elevate yourself, to seek a knowledge of yourself through enlightenment.

This is accomplished through disciplining the body until it obeys you, disciplining the mind until it stops resisting you, becoming disciplined in spirit.

Once you achieve this you experience a profound joy that is a 100 times greater than the temporary, body at risk fact of the Joy of Combat.

With the Joy of Combat you become a fighter.

In subduing the Joy of Combat, fighting becomes secondary to analyzing a situation and responding with the correct moves.

Life balances and harmonizes.

You begin to feel a joy within that is akin, but sharper and more profound, than the satisfaction of a job completed.
You begin to realize that yourself, as a spirit, is actually a joyful thing. You begin to live life as
a gift and a blessing.

The idea of putting on gloves to dominate somebody, or to 'prove you are better,' or some other aberrant concept, becomes abhorrent.

Chapter Seventy
Winning 100% of the Time

I began doing Rhythmic Freestyle to defeat the Joy of Combat. I quickly realized that I had stumbled on something big.

The first time I did freestyle the instructor put me in a stance and said, 'Try to block me.'

He then proceeded to lambast me, to wail on my hide, to beat holy heck into me.

Oh, he was gentle, but within five minutes I was frustrated beyond belief.

And he was a bully.

Oh, yes, that method works, if the individual is hardy enough, but teaching by giving somebody continual and abundant losses is not a good method of teaching.

Yes, mistakes teach, but we are talking about a procedure, not just an attitude towards life.

In Rhythmic Freestyle the partners take turns blocking and striking.

THEY DO NOT GO FAST!

They flow, gently, and if one partner strikes another, the partner who did the striking is at fault, for the purpose of this drill is to teach the other guy how to block.

It is not how to fight, it is to teach somebody else how to block.

If they don't block, or block wrong, then you screwed up. You didn't teach them.

Giving the student the viewpoint of the teacher is a HIGHLY ELEVATED method of teaching.

And, here is the mathematics of the situation.

Two guys freestyle. If they are evenly matched, they will each suffer 50% losses.

But when you do Rhythmic Freestyle both students achieve 100% wins!

Nobody ever loses!

This is a VERY pure way to input information into a student.

After a few months, as little as ten or twelve hours, the student will automatically become elevated. He will make the move into regular freestyle TEN TIMES FASTER than in the normal method. furthermore, he will start to turn on his intuition, which is the point of all the training.

Chapter Seventy-One
Relaxing During Combat

There are so many people that push the idea of rage as a motivation, that one must emotionally charge themselves up for a fight.

In the true art one relaxes. When somebody offers me conflict I actually become calmer.

Simply, I have trained myself to look at combat, at threats aimed towards myself, so long and hard that when it happens I simply kick into the 'watching' mode.

Sometimes people think I am not alpha enough, or that I am some sort of Fabian. Nothing could be further for the truth.

The fact is that when people start looking at me for a fight, I begin analyzing, calmly and cooly, towards victory.

When they become excitable and throw frantic blows, I get ever calmer, and utilize precise blocks and strikes.

When they are flying off the handle, I am gripping the handle firmly.

The real art is not in fighting, it is in learning how to relax enough in the face of a fight that you don't become emotionally involved, but rather manifest a precise scientific method of subduing the situation.

What this means is that fights rarely happen to me, or even in my presence.

What happens is that I start handling the proposed fight on subtle levels that a person trained merely 'to fight' doesn't understand.

In other words, people who are emotionally upset, or charged in some manner, can't analyze a situation, and so have no hope of handling it, and so become easy fodder for my analytical calmness that pervades the situation.

The way to achieve this state of mind of which I am speaking is to simply do the forms, practice the techniques, putting your attention of riding yourself of distractions by making your body move in the most efficient manner possible.

If you can make your body achieve that efficiency, so can you your mind.

Chapter Seventy-Two
On Stopping Training

I have people approach me ALL the time wanting to start martial arts training…again.

They studied when they were ten, twenty, whenever, and they are sorry they didn't continue.

Now they are thirty or forty, have wasted time, could have been improving themselves on all levels, but, instead, their uniforms hang in the closet, pressed, their last belt draped around the neck of the hanger.

And they feel this deep regret.

Something they loved, that actually loved them back in the most unconditional manner possible, was put by the wayside.

Often they don't know why.

Sometimes it is, 'we didn't have the money,' or 'my father wanted me to play baseball,' or some other simple thing.

But money comes and goes, you just go earn more, learn to budget, and don't give up the things that you like, that improve you on your life's path.

And baseball, or hockey, or basketball, or whatever, are nothing more than behavior modification.

'Learn to get along.' 'Shake hands after losing.' 'it's not important whether you win or lose.

These old saws are fine, workable to a certain degree, but don't apply to the person who is going beyond the behavior modification and personal gratification of sports to a higher goal.

They don't apply to the artist.

Of course you should do that stuff. But the sports themselves are flawed, and the feelings they engender, 'beat the other team at all cost and here's your reward in the form of money and girls and whatever,' are false.

The only true feeling is learning the fine mechanics of the body, so you can temper the excesses of the mind, so that you can appreciate yourself, and humanity, on a spiritual level.

If I'm good, it's not because I'm good, it's because I didn't quit!

Chapter Seventy-Three
Doing Everything at 101%

Always produce 101%.

If the sensei asks for 100 kicks, give him 101.

If the teacher asks for ten pages of homework, give him eleven.

If your mother asks you to empty the garbage, mow the lawn, too.

This is not a matter of succumbing to 'authority,' but of choosing what kind of person you will be in life.

And it starts, is best and most easily expressed, on the mat.

If the coach wants you to practice bridging to escape the mount 50 times…do it 51 times.

It just makes you better.

This attitude improves your spirit.

When other people are groaning and saying, 'Oh, that's too much, I'm so tired,' you are practicing saying, 'Oh, this is fun, I can do more, I have more energy, I am above groaning and moaning, I'm going places!'

Secret of life: before you do a job you have to learn what that job is about. People who learn joyfully, with no emotional bushwah, learn faster, impress the boss, more, get the higher paying jobs, get the more beautiful girls (handsomer guys).

People who whine and cry, who try to get out of work, end up on the bottom rung. They are the ones who end up wondering why they get passed by. Why they don't have enough money. Why it takes them so long to get their next belt.

Again, it starts on the mat. But, more important, it starts in you, with your decision.

What kind of a person do you want to be?

Chapter Seventy-Four
Doing Everything at 1% Less

Figure out how to accomplish your task with 1% less energy.

You have to mow the lawn, figure out a better pattern so you can do it in 99% of the time. As the weeks pile up, the percents go lower, and you become extremely fast and efficient.

And…you turn out a better product.

The mat is the BEST place to figure this out.

Kick the bag hard. Watch it bounce. Make yourself more efficient in your motions so that the bag moves further when you kick it softer.

When you are teaching somebody, try to figure out how to speak in concepts, with less words. Try to frame the thought you are sharing with the least amount of words.

Instead of saying, 'you need to turn you foot so the hip turns so that more weight will be put into your kick,' say, 'Turn foot for more hip weight.'

Make things so simple they can be understood…and can't be misunderstood!

Eliminate long and lengthy discussions and focus on the concept.

I call this 'One sentence teaching.' And it should be 'One word teaching.' The one word being the exact concept needed for the student to get it.

This is the heart of the 'Economy of Motion' concept: Do the least and get the most.'

Funny thing, if you adhere to this you will eventually begin to perceive people's thoughts before they manifest. You will understand what people are saying before they have said more than two words.

You just become efficient in your thoughts.

Become efficient in the disciplining of your motion through the martial arts.

This leads to disciplining the mind to shut up.

Which reveals the true you.

And the true you has abilities that mere mortals can only dream of.

Figure out how to explain a whole concept
in the fewest words possible.

Chapter Seventy-Five
Moving Slowly

I began Tai Chi in the seventies, right around the time I got my black belt, and have never looked back. Absolutely phenomenal art.

Unfortunately, it is couched in mysticism, as are so many of the martial arts.

Mysticism comes from the word mystery, which means you simply don't understand something.

You can defeat mysticism with a good dictionary.

As the years went on I began applying Tai Chi concepts to other arts, and here is a trick:

The slower you go the more you look,
the more you look the more you know.

I used to write a short phrase on my palm. I would open and close my hand quickly, and ask students what was written. They would blink and scratch their heads and complain that it was too fast.

Sometimes they would say, 'Do it again!' To which I would reply, 'The universe never repeats itself.'

I would then open my hand slowly, and make the point that if you move slowly, you can better understand what is happening.

I began using this principle in all my arts.

I would take hours to go through a simple tai chi form.

I would take twenty minutes to go through a twenty move karate form.

But then I would understand.

I would understand things about the angles, things about shifting weight, things about how to relax the mind so you can focus on what you are doing.

Eventually I wrote the book 'Chiang Nan,' in which I translate Karate into Tai Chi Chuan.

Chapter Seventy-Six
Picking Partners

If you pick partners who are better than you, you have a better chance of learning.

If you look for the partner who is not as good as you will not learn as much.

This is such a simple thing, and yet I have to say it, there are people who don't understand this.

I constantly see people who pick partners in training because they like them.

Yet if you pick the person you don't like, you will learn to like him, and that will make you a bigger person.

I see people pick partners because they are the 'right size.'

Yet the person they will meet on the street will often be the 'wrong size.' They will especially be bigger, because bullies don't pick on people who look like they can beat them up, and, being afraid, which is part of being a bully, the bully perceives bigger people as being able to beat them up. So they pick on smaller people.

So pick a partner bigger, tougher, faster, stronger, and learn how to handle a real situation.

And when you fail, when you are trounced on the mat, don't just accept it. Even if the guy is a jerk, go to him, ask him what he did, how you can get better.

This appeals to the 'bigger person,' inside that fellow who just beat you. He likes being an authority, and it won't be long until he is sharing secrets, telling you things he learned over time, but is giving to you merely because you are appreciative and interested.

And, here's the real, great glory of this trick: if he is the sort of person you didn't like, you will find that you begin liking him.

Even when I was a white belt, I would try to arrange my position in class so that I would end up being paired with a higher belt, preferably a ranked black belt.

And when the command came to pair up I would quicker than spit turn to a high ranking belt and say, 'I know I don't know much, but can you help me?'

Boy, did I get some GREAT lessons!

Chapter Seventy-Seven
Appreciate ALL Martial Arts!

There is no art so bad that it can't be made good by a good martial artist.

There is no art so good that it can't be made bad by a bad martial artist.

So don't look down on that 'McDojo,' it has purpose in the scheme of things.

Actually, I began in a McDojo. And if it hadn't been for that phoney, baloney BS I wouldn't have ended up spending my life pursuing the art.

Sure, I had a false sense of myself, I was air kicking too much, I didn't have any real idea of how the world worked.

But it was a step in the right direction. And I managed to take a second step, and a third, and….

And this means to appreciate ALL martial artists!

I remember reading the old Bruce Tegner books, many long years ago. Then I got into the martial arts, and I began looking down on them for their simplicity.

One day I was talking to an advanced belt, and he spoke about how much the Bruce Tegner books helped him. How the simplicity of the drills made him aware of…concepts.

So I got a few of those old books and reread them, this time with an open mind.

Sure enough, though the drills were silly, the techniques unusable, I found a depth of concept in almost every single chapter.

It changed the way I wrote, the way I described the art.

And I'd like to think it made me a better person.

But only after somebody gently opened my mind, and showed me how to appreciate ALL martial artists.

Remember, even if some guy is a bozo, he might, even by accident, say the one thing that will ignite your imagination, cause you to learn something, make you a better person.

You simply can't buy into the notion that every single person on earth is not, underneath it all, a spirit, a human being, and possessed of all the depth of imagination in the universe.

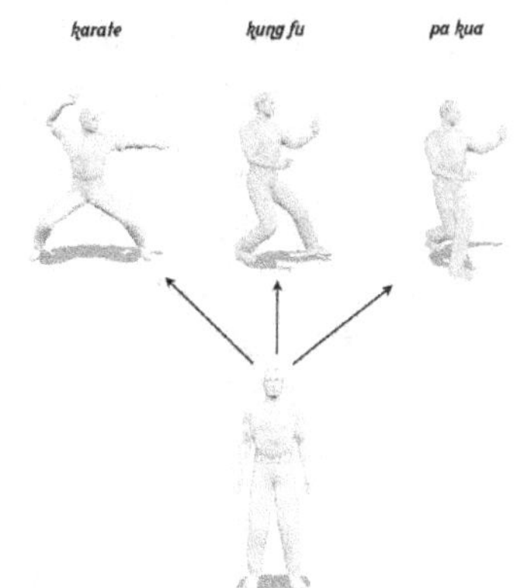

Chapter Seventy-Eight
Bowing

I find that bowing is misunderstood, totally and thoroughly, yet it is such a crucial part of being a human being.

A bow is a communication, and where would we be without communication?

The problem is that we have people who demand the bow as a form of domination. The bows are rigid, militaristic, and shade the whole practice fo the martial arts.

This is especially odious in competitions, when people scream as they bow.

A bow is a simple 'hi.'

You should bow when you enter a school.

You should bow when you step on to the mat.

You should bow to an opponent.

You should bow after a point in freestyle.

You should bow before asking a question.

You should bow to senior students.

You should bow after receiving instruction.

You should bow when leaving the mat.

You should bow when leaving the school.

You should bow whenever you feel like communicating.

You are not bowing down like a dog, if done rightly; you are saying 'hi!' Brightly and cheerfully, and establishing a base for further communication. Or, you are ending a communication.

Think about it: you are just saying hi. You are saying hi to individuals, to people who studied generations ago, to any and everybody to whom you wish
to offer respect and kindness.

And, as to the 'odious in competitions' remark I made a few paragraphs ago: Isn't it sort of silly to scream 'hi' to people, your body as rigid as ice? Isn't that a silly way to greet and announce?

Better to just say 'hi,' grin, and go about your business.

Chapter Seventy-Nine
Art Versus Science Versus Sport

There is science, and there is art. And, just as an aside, there is also sport.

Sport is when you are trying to beat somebody, this tends to bleed into the joy of combat. Though there can be much science in sport, it does not make it an art. And only rarely does sport make it to art.

Then there is art, wherein one expresses oneself, attempts to come in contact with one's spirit, and the opponent would be considered to be the self, that portion of the individual which needs to be subdued that the higher individual may evolve.

Science is the analysis of motion that one may become more efficient.

In art this aids the upward path.

In sports, this aids the beating of fellow men for gold and glory. Which often translates as pursing the Joy of Combat.

Sports is competition for competition's sake.

Science is the accurate measuring of endeavor.

Art is the expression of self.

Mind you, I am not saying sports is wrong, or one must adhere to science; I am merely defining the fields that one may better understand them, and make better decision regarding them.

What you do, and the level at which you do it, is up to you.

versus

Chapter Eighty
Domination in Teachers

One of the worst contraptions in the martial arts is the teacher who is into domination.

He demands you bow super low and with intense admiration, and he always talks about how you have to have 'respect.'

Has anybody ever considered that in his militaristic domination he shows you little respect?

The very word 'respect' has almost become a dirty word in this society.

It is a way of forcing friendship and admiration. But how can you force things like these?

Doesn't friendship, and admiration, have to be earned? And that through the manifestation of virtues that engender such responses?

Look, I have made myself clear on the fact of bowing, and saying 'hi' whenever you can, but when somebody makes me say 'hi' through forceful behavior I usually roll up my tent and head home.

I just don't want to rub elbows with people who believe in strict hierarchies of people defined by forced behaviour.

I only believe in the handshake and the grin.

Mind you, don't get me wrong, I run a tight class, I even raise my voice and bully people, but that is only to the purpose of making sure they hear me, that they get the instruction, that the discipline of the martial arts works for them.

As for domination...that's for weak minded individuals of low self-esteem who have little to teach and paltry character.

Helpful? 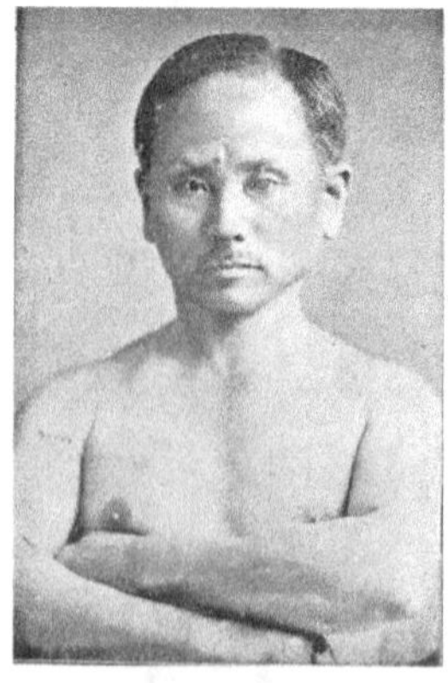 Or harmful?

Chapter Eighty-One
Seeking to Instruct

Teaching is a blessing.

Teaching teaches the teacher.

One often has to work ten hours just to teach for one hour. Once one has become established this doesn't have to be true, but it usually is in the beginning.

The reason teaching is so great is because it cements in the mind of the teacher the principles and concepts of the dojo.

The dojo is a microcosm, a smaller universe inside the larger universe, and if you can learn martial principles and concepts in this smaller universe, they become easier to implement in the larger universe.

When you show a student how to angle his foot correctly, you are more likely to adhere to having the correct foot angle yourself.

If you discuss how to implement martial principles with a student or students, you are going to be better at implementing martial art principles in your own life.

Teaching is a chance to lead, a chance to share knowledge, to make others better, to improve the march of humanity through the ages, to enable all of mankind to trod the upward path to enlightenment.

Good teaching is what you wish had happened to you so that you didn't make all those mistakes.

It is for these reasons, and more, that I encourage everybody to, in some fashion or other, in some field or other, become a teacher.

Chapter Eighty-Two
Master of All Arts, Jack of None

There is an old saying, 'Jack of all trades, master of none.' This is to say that one should not spread himself too thin, that one should not be so interested in all things that he fails to focus on, and master, one thing.

While there is a certain amount of truth to this concept, in the martial arts it cannot be applied.

Yes, you should specialize in one art, focus on it, master it, but you should also study all arts.

You must absorb information from all arts, every spectrum, all ranges, and condense it so that the martial arts become one field.

To study only one art is to limit your responses, and to lack understanding in the variety of ways a situation can be dealt with.

To study one art to mastery, then acquaint oneself, in depth, with all arts, is to understand that a single art is but a slice of the whole, and it is the whole that you should be focused on, and that mastering a single art is but a single step towards mastering the whole.

There was a fellow in Japan, a high ranking Karate black belt, who was admired by all for his high understanding of art.

One day he packed up and moved to China. Decided to study Tai Chi Chuan. He spent ten years mastering Tai Chi Chuan, and other Karate instructors curled their lip, figured he had gone off the rails, that he was a betrayer and not really sincere in his study of art.

After ten years he returned home and resumed studying and teaching Karate.

Now all the other instructors applauded him, welcomed him back to the true martial art and the true path.

He ignored all, before, during and after. He was only concerned with the study of karate all along, but he knew he wouldn't truly understand it unless he approached it from a different point of view.

He was the true martial artist, he was the true master, and he had the true understanding. The fellows who sneered and looked down upon him, their art was weak.

Chapter Eighty-Three
What is Zen?

When I began Karate, back in the 60s, there were no movies, no books, no magazines. In the search for martial arts knowledge I came across this thing called Zen.

Pored over 'Zen Flesh, Zen Bones.' Began educating myself as to directly experiencing, versus talking about.

And that is a huge difference.

Do you know? Or know about?

Have you ever been immersed in the ocean? Or have you merely seen pictures of it?

In 'Zen and the Art of Archery' Eugene Herrigle demonstrates this difference so that you can know, not 'know about,' what zen is.

Ultimately, zen is knowledge gained through direct experience. There is no other zen.

Zen specializes in creating space about the individual.

In that space one has existence, and begins to understand that the universe is built of emptiness (an illusion). One begins to understand that the body is an illusion.

In the martial arts one practices the forms, the techniques, and directly experiences an expansion of space and existence.

It is difficult, because there are always bozos who run around and claim that if you don't beat somebody up it's not real.

But you practice the forms until they are real. You practice the techniques until they are intuitive. Then you don't have to fight.

The space about you is purified, and those who wish to fight wane and disappear when they enter your space.

Just remember: discipline yourself through the forms until you control them, and they don't control you.

Seek to do the forms without distraction, and you will enter a zen state of mind: you will perceive the universe directly, and you will not be fooled by it.

Chapter Eighty-Four
Do the Art Until the Art Does You

At first you practice in confusion, trying to remember the moves, trying to understand what you are doing, a picture in clumsiness and forgetfulness.

As time goes on you become expert, and you polish your art to higher and higher extremes.

Eventually you enter this state of intuition. Mushin no shin, the Japanese call it. Mind of no mind.

You have put away your mind, that collection of memories that trap and ensnare you, that trip you up and make you make mistakes.

You put aside normal methods of dealing with life and begin using intuition.

One day, I was working in a dimly lit and noisy warehouse, a fellow tried to sneak up on me.

I happened to be showing a fellow how to use a sword, and I was holding a piece of track using for sliding doors.

Suddenly, I felt a huge hand grab me and turn me, and force my upraised piece of track downwards.

I cut the fellow who was trying to sneak up behind me, ripping a jagged line down his chest.

It was only the fact that some piece of me knew that something was amiss, that made me resist the giant hand with all my might, that saved the fellow's face from major disfigurement.

I had been true in my study of art, and the art protected me.

There is a spirit that is greater than a human in a body.

You are not just eyes and ears and bits of conglomerated flesh, put together for the purpose of tripping about the planet in uncoordinated fashion.

You are your imagination, you are a sense in all directions, you perceive without the need for eyes and ears, and you perceive in 360, the center of a sphere.

If you sat in a tub of water, eyes closed, and sensed the movement of water as something entered the tub, that is similar to the feeling of being protected by the art.

You perceive in all directions, and to the finest degree necessary. That is what the art teaches you.

Chapter Eighty-Five
Finding Your True Opponent

You learn, courtesy of family and educators and that manner of people, to fight back.

Or, in today's liberal society, you learn not to fight, which makes you nothing more than a helpless, and sometimes hopeless, victim.

But if you are raised 'properly,' you learn to stand up, to make yourself heard, to fight back at those who would oppose you.

You fight to be the top grade in school.

You fight to be the one promoted.

You fight to reign in the ring, in the workplace, in the community.

But, in such fighting, which is really just a manifestation of the Joy of Combat, you never find your true opponent.

Who is it that stops you from reaching the top?

From getting the highest grade?

From being promoted over others?

It is yourself.

It is the demons within who nag and cause self-doubt.

A man without demons rises straight to the top.

But what are…who are…those demons?

They ARE the self-doubt.

Self doubt had to exist before you bought into it.

Self doubt was in you, and you raised it up merely to explain your lack of purpose.

To refuse the self-discipline necessary to do the hard work.

You are your true opponent.

It is defeating your base parts, and elevating your good character, that is the battle.

It is a sorry fact: you can tell a man to kill a tiger, and he will bring that tiger to the table, legs straight up. But if you tell a man to understand himself he will climb up on that table and lie with his legs straight up.

Chapter Eighty-Six
Share Knowledge and Create Understanding

Back to teaching.

Whenever you teach you are trying to get an idea out of your head and into somebody else head.

This is so simple, and yet so few are able to do it.

Either the idea they attempt to share is ill formed, tainted by aberration, odd, in some manner, or the person they are attempting to give that idea to is resistant, has odd ideas of his own getting in the way, or is, in some fashion, putting up barriers that that information dare not cross into his own experience.

This is why I adhere to 'one sentence teaching' as a way to impart single concepts. I keep it simple so that the ideas will be be confused and misunderstood.

And I let the forms speak for themselves.

Mind you, I have made the forms scientific through my study of matrix logic, and this has made the forms ever more important in the transmission of knowledge from me to another.

Once that knowledge is imparted in correct fashion, and the student has it, he will have more understanding. He will, at least, understand you.

If your understanding is good and true, he will benefit.

But even if your understanding is weak, at least he will have one more viewpoint to inspect on the way to finding his own viewpoint...his own truth.

This is the point of it all: not just to teach, but to teach with the idea of creating a better, more fuller and rounded person.

When you share knowledge you create understanding, and that makes a better world.

And, to the extent that the world is a mess, filled with wars and devious personalities, to that extent have people failed to share knowledge and create understanding.

If there was universal understanding there would be no wars, no intolerance, no murder and rape and poverty... pandora's box would be closed, and all the ills contained.

Chapter Eighty-Seven
Facts Over Opinions

First, never let a fight happen.
If you have, you have fallen to a lower level.

Second, ignore people who speak ill of one art over another. These are ignorant people looking to start fights.

Third, ignore people who speak ill of anything.

The old saw, if you don't have something nice to say…don't say anything at all, applies.
To pay attention to people who speak ill is to open the mind to negativity.
The fact is that people who speak ill invariably have no direct experience.
They are speaking because 'they've heard,' or because they have some set idea which doesn't apply to the situation at all.

There is a difference between some fellow who says, 'I studied art XYZ, and I found it didn't focus on weapons enough for what I wanted,' and the fellow who says, 'They're bad, they're a McDojo.'
One guy has experience, the other fellow is repeating rumor.
If you want to have a solid, stable life, in the martial arts and beyond, you have to follow one simple rule:

Place facts over opinions!

Never listen to rumor, and if you do hear one, ask for facts, ask for why that opinion has been reached, get to the bottom of the matter.

Guaranteed, your life will work 100% better if you do this.

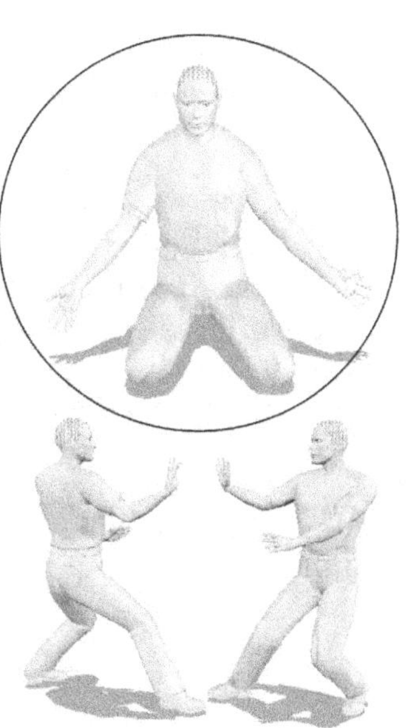

Chapter Eighty-Eight
The Eyes Have It

Always look people in the eye.

Simply, you can't fight what you can't face.

You can't even understand what you can't face.

There was a fellow in Indonesia who walked around squeezing hot peppers on his naked eye. He was trying to force his eyes to stay open, not to cry, not to even blink.

Well, maybe we've gone a bit too far, in this example, but the point is made.

The eyes are the windows to a man's soul, and if you are really going to get anywhere in this life you have to open your soul, you have to let people in, and trust that your discipline has made you, the soul, hardy enough to experience what life has to offer.

In fact, one of the most interesting things I ever came across was the idea that eyes are like flashlights, actually giving off beams of light.

I actually subscribe to this.

I have experienced the piercing gaze that made one turn around, both from others, and my own efforts.

I have met people eye to eye in such a way that we were timeless, beyond body, spirits meeting without the bushwhacked of memory and all that sort of baggage.

I have experienced 'mind to mind' communication, which is actually a poor description because the mind is memories, and it is not the minds that are communicating, but the spirits.

This ability can easily be cultivated through the hard core discipline of the martial arts.

Simply do the forms, learn to relax, and the world will eventually become tubelike. When you focus on something the world will fade and it will be like you are in a tube; you will be experiencing directly; watching like a spirit.

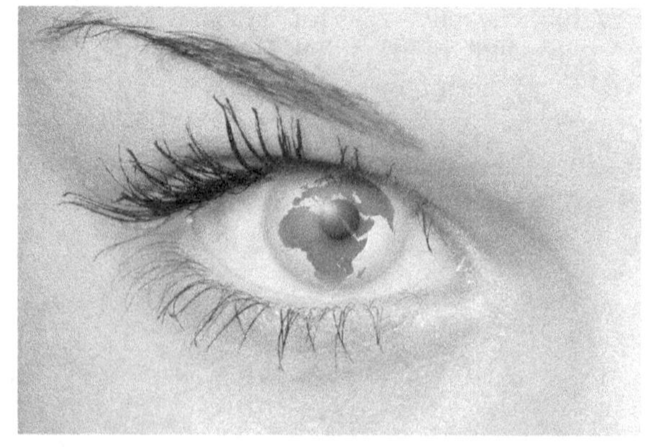

Chapter Eighty-Nine
Entering the Tube

I first became aware of this 'tube' of awareness when I asked my instructor if he he ever had anything mystical happen to him.

My motivation was simple, I had begun experiencing mystical things.

He told me that he had been freestyling, and suddenly it was like he was 60 feet above, looking down at himself as if through a long tube.

Still, I was not experiencing this myself.

But I kept doing my forms, doing my techniques, and, interestingly enough, it began to happen in freestyle.

Mind you, it didn't happen because of freestyle. If I had depended on fighting for my illumination I never would have experienced the tube.

It was the forms, it was focusing on my techniques, it was looking at what I was doing, trying to understand everything by analyzing what was really happening.

Then, after many years, I realized that when I was focusing on an opponent the world was fading away; there was only myself and my opponent.

The tube didn't waver, it became more solid as I focused my efforts on creating it.

And, I began to see what people would do before they did it.

By relying on that false mechanism, just a bunch of memories, called the 'mind,' I learned nothing.

It was only when I went beyond the need for eyes and ears and biomechanics mechanisms that I realized the truth: man is not flesh. He is not eyes and ears. The eyes and ears, and all the other senses, are merely objects through which we look.

The real question is: what is doing the looking?

And the answer is: The 'I am.' The spirit. The awareness that directs all things.

Nothing in the world happens unless the 'I am' tells it to.

Unfortunately, people are so asleep they don't know that they are an 'I am,' let alone how to function as one.

The martial arts, if they are properly done, and that means learning matrixing logic and neutronic philosophy, does.

Chapter Ninety
Using the Tube

Imagination is your greatest tool. It is what separates you from the animals, it is a factor generated by the spirit.

I had been doing Tai Chi Chuan for some twenty years, and I knew a taste of what the books claimed for the benefits and abilities for Tai Chi, but I decided I was taking too long. So I decided to speed things up.

At one point in my training I had viewed the world as geometry. I had envisioned the body in shapes, as constructions of triangles, squares and circles.

And I had imagined my strikes as never ending projections of energy, as arcs and slices that would cut to the stars.

I applied these methods to Tai Chi, and then I stumbled across the method by which I would move to the head of the class.

I would do Tai Chi in my backyard. I would close my eyes, and imagine I was looking down from 50 feet overhead.

Sometimes it was difficult, my mind would fuzz up, my focus couldn't hold the image of myself, I would get confused as to which I was moving, my body or my mind.

But I kept at it, and my perceptions all changed.

I began to look at people as if from far away.

I achieved a bigger sense of myself.

One day I was driving and I felt like I was extending myself through the mechanics of the car and could actually grip the road, the tires my fingers, the motor breathing in concert with me.

I began to feel like people were putty in my hands, and I could do what I wished with them.

Really, one doesn't get outside oneself unless one sets up an exercise like this.

Chapter Ninety-One
A Point in All Directions

One day I was practicing martial arts with a friend named Bruce.

Specifically, we were practicing 'Sticky Hands,' a drill from Wing Chun Kung Fu, but which we had learned in Karate, which Bruce Lee did.

There we stood, arms intertwined, going through the motions, trying to figure it out.

Mechanically, I understood it.

Find the central place for the elbows, let the pressure of the opponent guide your arms in guiding his strikes.

Then I had an idea: what if I balanced my arms? What if I balanced the flow of energy through each arm?

So I focused, became aware of energy, put equal amounts in each arm, balanced them on the centerline of my body, which came out of the tan tien.

Pop. Nothing fancy or crazy, I was suddenly aware from a spot behind my head.

I, the spirit, the awareness of awareness, the 'I am,' was out of my body.

My body froze. It was as if I was in the grip of a huge hand.

Bruce froze, couldn't move, as if he was in the grip of a huge hand.

We stood there, frozen, me totally out of my body; a disembodied 'intelligence' (an awareness).

Terror whelmed me! I didn't know what I had done! I didn't know how to get back in my body!

Bruce's eyes were huge!

So I punched him.

It was like a Mac truck ran through his chest. He flew back a dozen feet, splatted against the wall, then fell to the ground.

"What did you do?" he asked, rubbing his chest.

But I didn't know; that was a knowledge that had yet to come, but which would be sought because of this experience.

An explanation had to be sought and formulated. But I tell you this:

A spirit, you, are a point in all directions.

But it is scary to become disembodied, to get out of your comfortable earthly 'envelope' of flesh.

Chapter Ninety-Two
The Truth of the Universe

One day I was sitting on my backyard. This was after several years of hard core discipline. Discipline in which I had practiced all I had been told, but had then put aside to further practice by my own lights. Lights which would eventually formulate into my 'Matixing' logic and 'Neutronic' philosophy.

I was sitting on a cinder block, tapping a piece of rebar on the concrete of the patio. Music was playing, 'The Horse with No Name' by America. Everything was beautiful, calm, peaceful.

Ting ting ting, I tapped the rebar. Ting ting Ting. Ting ting…TO-O-ONG!

It was like a golden bell, the echo receding into infinity. The world was golden. The trees were alive such as I had never seen them. Even the particles in the air glowed with spirit. And I realized:

**For something to be true
the opposite must also be true.**

It was the truth of the universe; it was enlightenment; it was the illumination of my soul, suddenly ignited, awake, beyond earthly convention and human contrivance.

I would spend my life understanding how that simple phrase described the universe and how it actually works.

I would spend my life figuring how to apply that to the martial arts.

It would justify, without need for explanation, my efforts to contribute to the martial arts: that people would awake through a simple discipline.

Oh, I wanted to be a writer before then, but now I knew what I wanted to write.

Yes, I have people who sneer at me, offer their silly criticisms, born out of their desire to protect themselves from the knowledge that they are more than the fleshy envelopes called bodies.

But when I say something crazy, when I talk about energy and spirit beyond body and remembering when I was a different person in a different time, when I talk about picking some stranger's mind and learning an art, understand that it is my experience, and that it can be yours. You just have to have the discipline…and the desire.

People who sneer and meanly laugh…they do so to protect their ignorance, and they have nothing to offer you except the chains of their thoughts and conventions.

Chapter Ninety-Three
Talking to Animals

Talking to animals? WTF does that have to do with the martial arts?

When you discipline yourself enough through forms and techniques, and do a modicum of freestyle, you become sensitive to your opponent's thoughts. You can tell when he is going to strike. Sometimes you can even tell what he is going to do.

As life goes on, and as the lessons of the microcosmic dojo radiate into the macrocosm of life, these abilities are felt in normal interactions with people.

Interestingly, it is easier to read animals minds, and can even act as a precursor to the human 'mind reading.'

Animals don't have as much verbiage, their barks and meows and chirps and such don't give them much of a database for nuance and inflection.

Thus, animals usually communicate more on the mental level, sending thoughts clean and easy.

Also, animals don't lie, which really makes it easy to understand…unless you are possessed of a lying personality. A lying personality isn't 'pure' enough to accept honest thoughts. The barrier of duplicity shields the mind from honesty.

The way to read animal minds is to simply create lots of silence in your life, and when you encounter an animal know that the first thought you receive will be the actual thought.

Past that, it is what you fantasize what an animal is thinking.

Picking up that first thought, you understand how to give back a thought: light, a flitter, nothing else.

And, animals don't repeat themselves. They will repeat the verbiage, a constant bark, for instance, but the thought has come and gone and the rest is all just manifestation of the thought.

I was walking down the street once, with a student, and we came to a yard with a vicious dog. It was a Doberman, and I saw it up the block, and I knew, instantly, that the animal liked to scare people.

We walked past the yard, and as the dog in took breath for a bark, I spun and kiai-ed. The dog ran in fear for its house.

My student almost ran away from me.

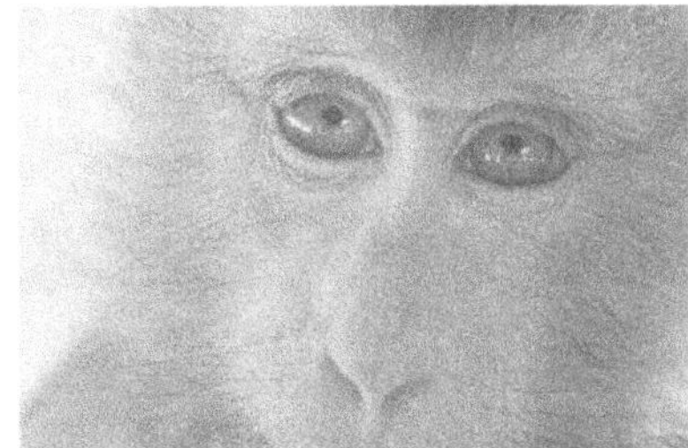

Chapter Ninety-Four
Tragedy is an Opportunity

Life is a waveform.

It goes up; it goes down. sometimes the magnitude of the wave fools us, not revealing when a particular upslope or downslope is going to be.

Thus, as life goes up and down, we must learn to climb or surf, as the need may be.

And not hang on to climbing when the wave tumbles, nor the surfing when the wave ascends.

The difficult thing to learn is that in the midst of the severe downslope, when tragedy tumbles us head over heels, when the world is filled with whining and moaning, that there is an opportunity.

When your house burns…you get to build a new one. And, guaranteed, good thinking people will come out of the woodwork and find themselves helping you.

When you lose a job…you get to find a better one! And bosses will vie with one another for the chance to utilize your skills.

When your wife dies? There is another one, a prettier, more accommodating one in the wings.

When your children are arrested for drug trafficking? The world is a better place!

Unfortunately, most people get hung up in their emotionalism, paying attention to their feelings, and not looking outward, searching for the opportunity.

The reason for this should become obvious as you read this book.

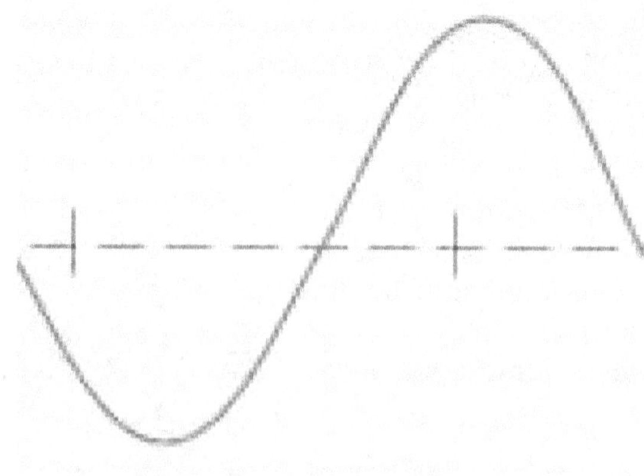

Chapter Ninety-Five
Enlightenment

Enlightenment is when the 'light' of realization floods through you, apprising you of the true state of the world, of your true state of mind.

Enlightenment can be realized in little steps, no big flash of lightening, but have as much, if not more, impact than the big lightening.

The enlightenment most sought after is the big flash of realization.

The heavens opening up and showering one with inspiration.

When I became enlightened I found all that inspiration handy. But the truth was a path filled with endless work outs, frustrations with inadequate teachings, people who didn't understand squat, and so on.

Thus, enlightenment can be a two-edged sword.

My enlightenment set me on a path of constant toil, with little earthly reward. But I would not trade the understanding I achieved past that enlightenment for ANYTHING!

The truth of the matter is that, as in anything, education is done step by step. First you learn the basics, then you learn how they tie together, then you learn combinations, then you learn…and the path is step by step.

And here is something you may not have known: the competence gained through walking the path is more important than the momentary flash of enlightenment.

That all said, I will tell you something else: enlightenment makes you realize that you are more than human, that you are a spirit, an 'I am,' an awareness of awareness.

With that enlightenment comes abilities.

The ability to dream, and to make that dream work.

The ability to communicate by thought.

The ability to know what people are thinking, before they do themselves.

And all manner of other abilities.

But the cost of those abilities is enormous.

The cost is increased responsibility, to those around you, and to the world at large.

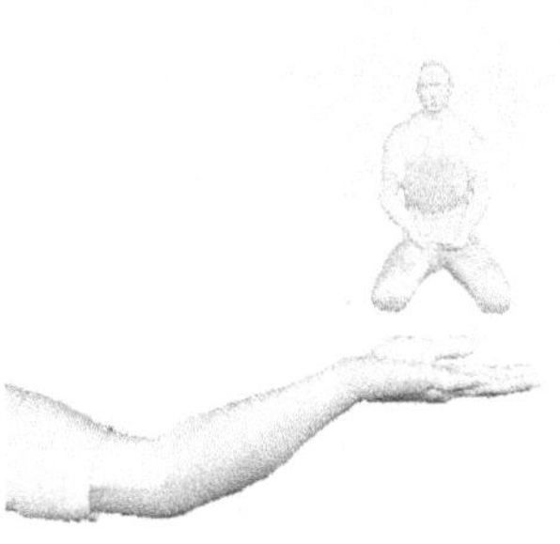

Chapter Ninety-Six
Dreams

When I was a child, a boy, a colored belt in the affairs of man, I had dreams.

These dreams were nothing more than the meanderings of my mind, excessive slop overcoming the rim of sleep and disturbing me.

At the time I received my black belt I dreamed of a tiger.

I talked to the tiger, and the tiger showed me how he moved. And I was aware within this dream.

I was no longer the victim of my daytime emotions, stirred to slop by my untidy personality; I was now aware within dreams, able to take advantage of the images, able to effect my path for the better.

At the time of this writing I have no dreams. My mind is at peace for the simple reason that I am in charge of it, and it no longer holds any sway over me.

My discipline has tamed me.

When I do have occurrences while sleeping they are not dreams, but aware adventures in the ether.

The ether is that substance of which the universe is built.

The ether is thought universes from which are constructed the things of the so called 'real' universe.

Everybody has their own (etheric) universe, and all (etheric) universes coincide, by two's usually, but can be the convergence of the whole of humanity's (etheric) universes.

The ether is the universe in which all decisions are made concerning the false universe in which we find ourselves having day to day existence in.

The etheric universe has no time.

It is very interesting to talk to Napoleon in the ether; there is no before or after, just the knowledge that he has existence as Napolean…when there is time.

The etheric universe is the idea from which all forms gain substance.

You might think I am talking nonsense now, but I realized, through the study of 'forms' in the martial arts (an etheric universe in its own right) what the 'forms' such people as Plato were when posited way back when.

And, believe me, direct experience of the universe, and of the ideas of the universe, formed in the ether, is so much better than anything modern education would espouse.

Fact, people who talk but have never experienced the ether should just shut up. They only confuse the matter.

Chapter Ninety-Seven
Which Way Does Man Go?

This is such an interesting question, especially since mankind is a 'race.'

Where do we race to, eh?

The fact is that a spiritual being has no direction. He is, at best, a point in all directions.

It is the universe that moves, and the universe is an illusion, something we built in which to have being.

And, forgetting that, we have become victim to our own creation.

Frankenstein-like, the universe shoves us around, and we think we are billiard balls and the cues of the gods, or worse, chance, move us about.

But we are not the screen upon which the movie is played, we are the projector playing upon the screen.

We move the universe, the universe is our creation, and it whims according to our whims, if we could only rid ourselves of verbiage and rely upon that very pure projection of thought.

So, that all being said, let us get to the crux of the matter: which way does man go?

He goes in or out.

If he is going out, he is not introverting, trying to play with the projector, but actively moving the chess pieces upon the board of the universe.

If he is going in he is messing with himself, masturbating, losing himself in the significance of the question: Am I?

Do you see?

The fellow who goes into the universe, shining his lights full force, moving the universe as he would a game board, is saying 'I am.'

The fellow who shrinks from the universe, thinks he is but a pawn upon the board, is saying 'Am I?'

This is simple to prove. Try to listen and speak at the same time.

Except for the glories of putting one or the other on automatic, you can only do one thing at a time.

You can either go in, or out, and there is no middle ground.

Such things as 'balance,' or 'harmony,' or other concepts heaven-like in nature, come about only through the actions of a human being who is manifesting himself outward, and placing the universe until it harmonizes, and balances, with the thoughts he has projected.

Chapter Ninety-Eight
Matrixing

Matrixing is the application of logic to the martial arts…and to life.

I began matrixing through the simple compiling of lists.

I would write every technique I knew.

I would try to categorize these techniques by force and by flow…and by various geometric artifice.

Eventually the lists became unwieldy; I couldn't make comprehensive lists of all the techniques I knew. There were just too many, there was just too much overlap between arts, and so on.

I began making little tables, according to geometric bent, and I began to notice things.

I began to find techniques that I hadn't known were there.

I began to find missing pieces of forms.

I began to see how martial arts were all slices of the same pie.

Eventually I began creating matrixes to describe these things I was seeing, and matrixing was born.

I was making lists of techniques all the way back to my days at the Kang Duk Won.

I began matrixing in the early eighties.

Oddly, I thought everybody was doing this. I was quite surprised when one of my students apprised me that this wasn't so.

So I began writing articles based on matrixing techniques, and found an instant home with CFW enterprises (Inside Kung Fu, Inside Karate, etc.)

Finally, I began making video tapes.

Seeing some of the early ones, all fuzzy with poor technology and a lack of technical knowledge, one can see that i was stumbling blindly.

Still, people began writing me letters, then emails, telling me how much Matrixing was effecting them, how they were looking at their martial arts in new and unprecedented ways, how they were finally understanding what the 'old masters' were saying.

I began MonsterMartialArts.com and things haven't been the same since.

I have students in dozens of countries around the world.

I get emails (over 600 pages of them) daily.

And I continue to discover new things using matrixing.

Matrixing has gone beyond the martial arts, been used in classrooms and in other endeavors than the martial arts.

Chapter One Ninety-Nine
Neutronics

Matrixing uncovered vast swaths of knowledge for me. Amongst the knowledge was knowledge of the self.

Matrixing is a grand scheme that organizes all motion and potential motion in the universe.

The spirit is not of the universe, and the definition and description of this spirit necessitated a different kind of logic, a philosophical logic. Neutronics came into being.

The universe is a dichotomy, built upon the simple dictum:

For something to be true
the opposite must also be true.

That which is spirit, not of this universe, also follows a simple dictum:

A point in all directions is no point at all.

Researching Neutronics I discovered such things as what the mind really is, what emotions really are (motion inside the head), and various other things having to do with the 'paranormal,' which is the real abilities of the spirit.

If Matrixing is the scribing of all potential motions in the universe, Neutronics is the analysis of motivations through the simple fact that a line goes in two directions.

Neutronics is the philosophy behind the logic of matrixing.

It is the genesis of motivation behind motion.

It is based upon the simple fact that an atom has two opposing (dichotomous) particles, the proton and the electron, but that the most important element of the atom, and analogous to life and the fact of the human spirit, is the neutron.

You can kill a body, but you can't kill a spirit.

Chapter One Hundred
Where Matrixing and Neutronics Lead

In the beginning one is stumbling along, memorizing things that don't work presented by teachers who don't know how to teach. Then you discover Matrixing.

Matrixing is basically a 'software program' for the mind. You do it, it's logical, it makes things easier, and the martial arts resolve.

Running a program like this has an interesting effect on the human being: he likes it. The mind likes what is simple, it likes what is intuitive, and the mind resolves. Thus, the second stage of matrixing is like correcting the computer.

You start to think logically. You apply matrixing to other fields. Suddenly, math isn't so hard, the English language starts to make sense. Other subjects become logical and easier to learn. You are starting to look beyond the surface and into the deeper parts of what it means to be a human being.

And, once you have straightened out your computer, and interesting things happens.

You start to read minds, sense what is going to happen before it happens, and…connect with other human beings.

This is like straightening out the 'server.' Other people like you, they like being around a person who makes sense, who isn't complex, who laughs easily and makes them feel good about themselves.

Unfortunately, all they are getting is the fringe.

To get the real benefits of Matrixing, and Neutronics, in the martial arts, one must become a teacher.

The teacher has the ultimate viewpoint. He is outside the action, even when he is in it, looking down a long tube and seeing exactly what is happening…before it even happens.

So I always encourage people to become not just teachers, but teachers of martial arts, of Matrixing, and of Neutronics.

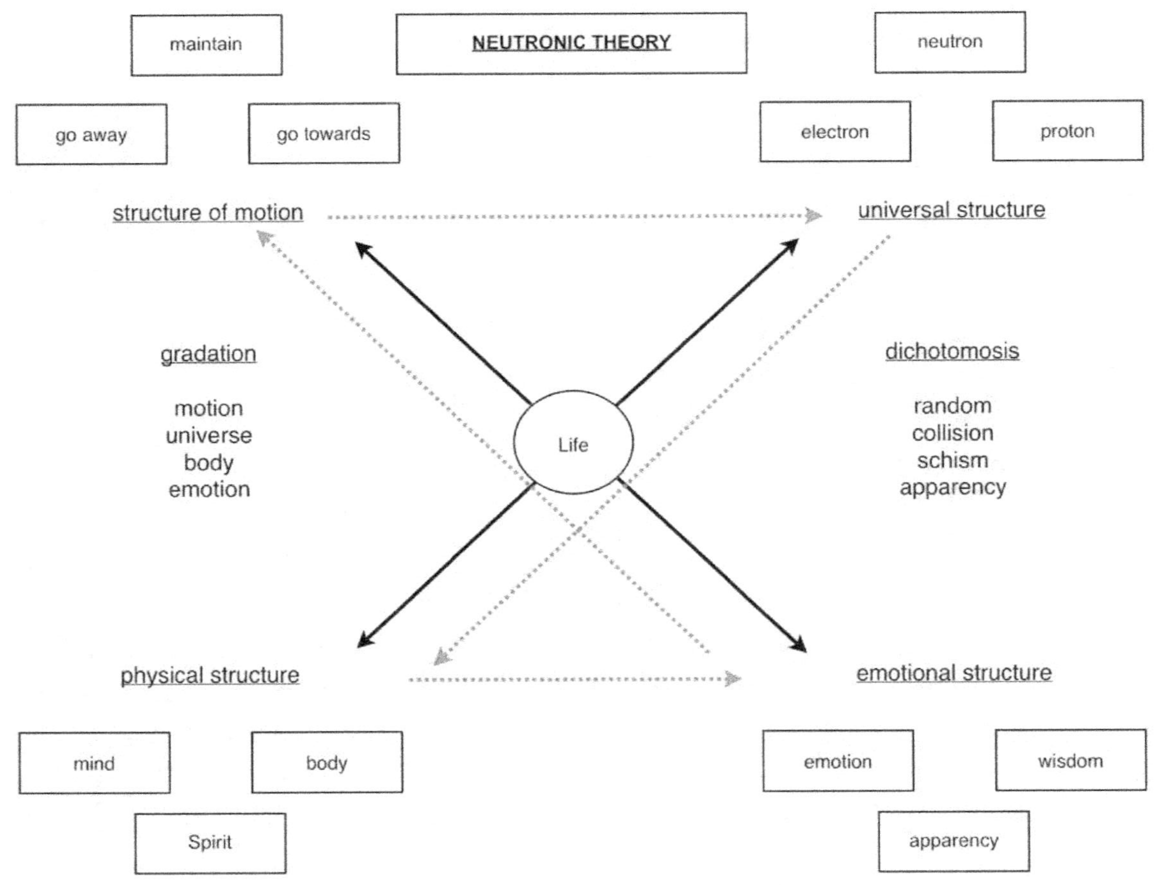

maintain
NEUTRONIC THEORY
neutron
go away
go towards
electron
proton
structure of motion
universal structure
gradation
motion
universe
body
emotion
Life
dichotomosis
random
collision
schism
apparency
physical structure
emotional structure
mind
body
Spirit
emotion
wisdom
apparency

Chapter One Hundred One
Myself

I am currently in a body that is 70 years old, but thinks it is 25.

I walked into my first martial arts school at age 19, in 1967.

Within five lessons I had mystical experience and knew that I would do the martial arts for the rest of my life.

I have studied everything I could concerning the martial arts, and have come into a lot of peripheral knowledge.

I have spoken of my experiences and arts in scores of books, and hundreds of hours of video.

What I haven't spoken of is what drives me.

I knew I wanted to be a writer from about the age of two. I remember seeing my father reading a pulpish paperback and knowing that I wanted to hold people's attention the way that book held his.

I just didn't know what I wanted to write about.

I hated school. It was regimentalism, an imprisonment in the ways of this universe. It was the indoctrination of my mind with scads of rules and false reasons.

Science is the measurement of the universe, but what good does it do to measure things?

Measuring things only enabled me to be a member of the species entrapped in this universe. It did nothing to free my spirit, or elevate my experience of life.

The martial arts changed all that.

Through the manipulation of form I found space; through space I discovered myself.

That which I had known all along was true, the universe being forced upon me was the lie.

In the end, that which drove me, which propelled me through the experiences and concepts you have read herein, was a desire not to be famous, but to write 'letters' to people who live a thousand years from now.

Those are my friends. Those are the people who do not judge me, but rather enjoy me.

125

THE SCIENCE OF MATRIXING
IN THE MARTIAL ARTS

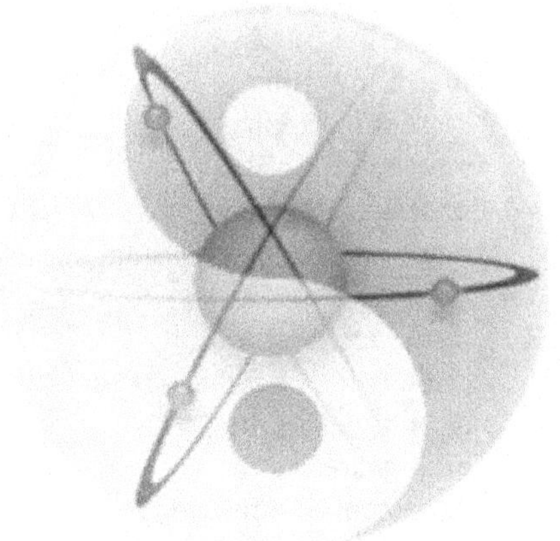

Table of Contents for Science of Matrixing

intro

Matrixing is the science of the Martial Arts. It is the ONLY science of the martial arts on this planet. It is logic applied, and results in an incredible philosophy of life that will enhance mankind into the ages.

There is the East, and there is the West.

The East provides an education that is lacking in linearity. Which is to say: it does not possess the logic of the West.

This is not a statement of good or bad, just of circumstance, for either culture provides a wealth of rich data to the individual who is willing to open his eyes.

In this book we will be exploring the concept of Matrixing (a form of Western logic) as it pertains to the East…and its fabulous systems of mysticism.

Specifically, we will apply logic to the Martial Arts.

In the Martial Arts, in Eastern methods, repetition of movement may result in a variety of mystical realizations, or experiences.

I say 'may' because most martial arts systems have become watered down, diluted, altered, and otherwise distracted from the purpose of leading an individual to realization. Which realization may include 'enlightenment.'

The western martial arts methods have become even more diluted, deviated and distracted from this goal. Often not even understanding the 'mystical' connection and how to achieve it.

Indeed, most western martial arts have degraded to boxing methods, providing a good 'work out,' as opposed to outlining a path to self-realization.

This book will go a long way towards returning the martial arts to the potential of the path of realization.

The logic of matrixing will define certain concepts, which will then become easier to understand.

Older training methods may again be embraced.

People will, at the very least, understand that there is something besides 'working the muscles.'

There is the individual; there is the unique 'I am;' there is hope.

Still, it depends on you using this material, understanding the logic, and then actually applying it.

It won't always be easy, because most people don't really embrace actual 'thinking.'

But it will be possible.

Good skill to you.

chapter one
What is a Matrix?

A matrix is a graph representing all potentials of motion, even including thought.

Once one understands all the potentials one is better able to make correct decisions.

The term matrix is derived from a Latin word relating to 'Mother.'

The reality of a matrix is that it was a cage used to contain female wolves, which were then used for breeding purposes.

A matrix came to represent certain mathematics.

Specifically, a matrix is a 'Truth Table,' which term comes from Boolean Algebra.

Boolean Algebra is used to describe three dimensional motions on two dimension surfaces.

For instance: 3D on a television screen, or a computer monitor.

In the Martial Arts this makes for a wonderful analysis of the motions of the body through the three dimensions of space.

And, more important, for the encapsulation and understanding of how the mind works, specifically to visualize (geometrically) the motion of the body through space.

This makes it VERY easy to grasp concepts of motion specific to the martial arts which may have been difficult to understand.

chapter two
Basic Theory

The basic theory of matrixing is very simple.

First, imagine yourself as a dot in space.

Not acted upon by gravity, nor even the 'leaning' of your thought.

Imagine nothing else in space.

Second, go to another spot.

This describes a straight line between two points.

Third, now realize that every line has two potentials. Towards or away. Positive or negative. Plus or minus.

This is the root of matrixing; this describes everything from the construction of the universe to how a spiritual being travels through space.

All that remains now is to ascribe those motions to a matrix.

And, the last word: the universe IS dichotomous. It has two 'sides.' These two sides are 'something,' and 'nothing.'

All something and nothing is constructed by awareness.

Thus, the universe is binary.

And everything in the universe is binary.

Atoms have positive protons and negative neutrons.

Cells have sodium and potassium.

Trees have tops and bottoms.

Human beings (and other 'animals') have a right and left.

And there is a forward and back, up and down, side to side, and so on.

BUT, there is invariably a third element. Not apparent in the construction of the universe, there is a is 'nothing,' which watches over everything.

On the macrocosmic scale we might call this a 'God' concept.

On a microscopic scale we would call this the human spirit. The 'I am' which is behind all that you are.

While you're thinking about all this stuff, let's look at our first Martial Arts matrix.

chapter three
Plus and Minus

	plus	minus
plus	plus/plus	plus/minus
minus	minus/plus	minus/minus

As stated, the universe is binary, a dichotomous construct.

However, the plus/minus and the minus/plus provide grey, or an 'in between.'

Thus, the universe has the potential for shades and even color.

Of course, these shades require finer and finer combinations of plus and minus to create the more brilliant hues.

For instance, in this table we have two inputs, and four potentials.

Take a look at the basic diagram from Pa Kua Chang (Eight Trigrams Palm Maneuvers) on the next page, which uses three inputs.

Notice that this diagram is grown from the simple yin yang, which is described by the fishes swimming in the center of the diagram.

Thus, two leads to eight trigrams, and, if you know anything about Pa Kua Chang, then you are aware that 8 leads to 64 palm changes, and a whole cosmogony of fire and thunder and earth and void and lightening and water and so on.

Which is to say....the universe.

But it all starts with understanding the basic matrix of Plus and Minus.

chapter four
Yes and No

	yes	no
yes	yes/yes	yes/no
no	no/yes	no/no

In the above matrix we have introduced the human element to a simple plus and minus.

Every human being has the ability, the right, the choice, to approve or disapprove of the basic direction they are involved in.

Without that ability we have a universe which is a machine, which is a trap, a cage, into which we are all inserted.

If you agree with a choice, if you wish to establish a direction, you simply say yes.

If you don't agree you simply say no.

BUT, if you say yes while thinking no, or no while thinking yes, your universe will have uncounted obstacles and barriers.

This IS the definition of life and how to live it.

To the degree that you are saying yes in a situation which you are thinking no, or saying no while thinking yes, to that degree you are trapped.

You are doing something you don't want to, and by going against your own thought you are going against life itself.

BUT, there is salvation.

Change your mind.

Go in the other direction.

It IS all a matter of direction…because it IS a binary universe.

This is actually all easy enough to understand.

When you were a kid you were told to do your chores, and you hated it, and you mouthed off to your parents, or worse, kept it all inside, and you became a mangled caricature of a free thinking, responsible and free human being.

What people don't realize is that freedom is a fickle thing.

To the degree that you take responsibility, to that degree you have freedom.

To the degree that you don't take responsibility, to that degree you DON'T have freedom.

It is really simple.

Yes or No. Do or Don't Do. Agree or Don't Agree.

A binary universe.

A binary universe made complex by your insistence in going against the directions you establish with your own day to day, moment to moment livingness.

So let me give you a basic formula.

For something to be true,
the opposite must also be true.

This is the yin yang verbalized.

With the understanding of the matrixes thus far presented, you may have hopes of understanding it.

Maybe even applying it.

Of course, you will have to reduce your viewpoint of life to the simple yes and no.

You will have to become binary in your thoughts.

And this is made ever so complex by the shades and hues of Positive and Negative that make up your life, are manifested by your own thoughts, and painted upon this canvas universe.

chapter five
Passive Aggressive

	towards	**away**
towards	towards/towards	towards/away
away	away/towards	away/away

The above matrix applies the plus and minus, the positive and negative, the yes and no, and all other manifestations of the simplicity of direction, to your life.

You wish to go towards someone, or away from them.
This is the source of all problems and all solutions.

A maniac with a knife in one hand and a gun in the other is coming towards you. Do you go towards or away?
A beautiful lady with lust in her eye is coming towards you. Do you go towards or away.
In reality, in the pureness of your universe, there are no shades or hues, no colors or distinctions.
Beauty is a made up something we use to judge the world, which separates us from living, and the reality of actually making decisions.
As is ugliness.

Can you avoid the trap of thinking black or white is a hue or color?
Can you see life for what it is? A simple urge for one direction or the other?
And, if you can, can you do it?
The answer is no. You can't.

You see, without the discipline there is only a wish, a dream.
Discipline is how you make the dream into reality.
Martial Arts are the discipline.

chapter six
Force and Flow

As stated in the beginning, the universe is constructed of something(s) and nothing(s).

The action of this universe consists of the flow of something (objects) through nothing (space).

In fact, there is nothing else except this flow of objects through space.

This leads to the theory of Force and Flow.

Flow is the trajectory of objects; force is when objects collide.

One can describe the actions of the martial arts, and even the strategy of managing the universe with the Force/Flow formula.

The purpose of the Martial Arts
is to deliver a Force or Flow
without receiving a Force or Flow

One can easily see how the earlier formula:

For something to be true
the opposite must also be true

…leads directly to the Force/Flow formula.

And the Force/Flow formula leads directly to the Purpose of the Martial Arts, which is essential to understanding and controlling, let alone commanding, the universe.

The purpose of the Martial Arts
is to deliver a Force or Flow
without receiving a Force or Flow

Here is the matrix that leads to the Force/Flow formula, which manifests the Force/Flow formula.

	force	flow
force	force/force	force/flow
flow	flow/force	flow/flow

chapter seven
Martial Arts

When one looks at the martial arts through the matrix viewpoint one sees that all martial arts are combinations and permutations of the Force/Flow graph presented in the last chapter.

Karate, on one extreme, might be considered to be Force/Force.

Aikido, on the other extreme, would be considered Flow/Flow.

Various styles of Kung Fu, Indonesian arts, and so on, would be combinations of Force/Flow and Flow/Force.

Consider the graph to the right.

A simplistic rendering, but it establishes a logical analysis of the Force and Flow developed, viewed, from a practice of the Martial Arts.

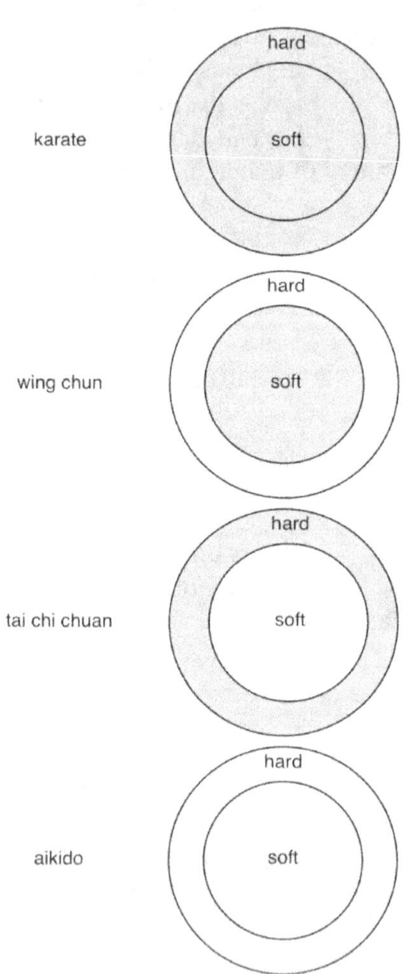

Another way of graphing this analysis of Martial Arts, stemming directly from the preceding graph, would be:

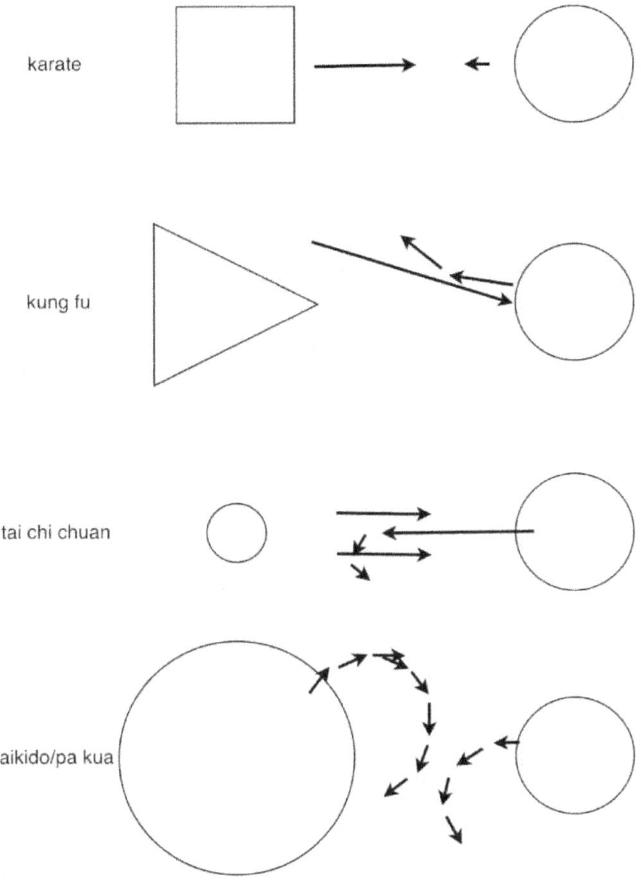

This is, again a simplistic analysis of the Martial Arts, there will be shades and hues and colors and anomalies galore when one actually achieves a complete mapping of the individual arts, and how they combine or 'get along with' other Martial Arts.

This leads us to yet one more step in this analysis.

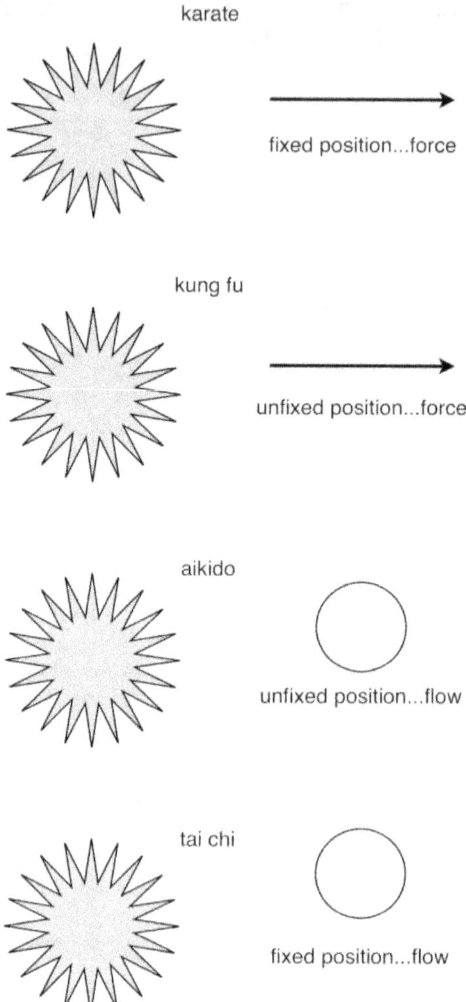

Thus begins the scientific resolution of motion and conflict within the Martial Arts.

To continue with this resolution, however, we must change tacks slightly and analyze the Martial Arts from further matrices having to do with such things as the individual weapons of the martial arts, distances involved, blocking and punching patterns, and so on.

chapter eight
The Whole Martial Arts

The Force/Flow formula, and the resulting matrices, clear away a plethora of significant misunderstandings in the Martial Arts. Here are just some of the misunderstandings, half truths, and other products of the mystical approach (especially when understanding is attempted by the 'scientifically' slanted Western mind.

People view Karate as a 'straight line' endeavor. It is considered a linear art, when nothing could be further from the truth.

To launch a straight punch entails a massive amount of curvature within the body.

The shoulder turns, the hips rotate…indeed, virtually every part of the human body is, in some manner, seeking a curve to launch a straight line.

There is often a dichotomy drawn between the straight line and the circle.

Hard and soft describe certain things, then the concept is 'leeched' and misunderstood for other things. Hard and soft more accurately represent the results of understanding the differences between force that is produced by effort, and force which does not entail effort.

There are separations drawn between striking and grappling, when the true science can be resolved by understanding how distance collapses in a fight.

There are separations drawn between all the various arts; stylistic considerations or viewpoints are held up as differences in the art, when they are really just complements.

To correct such misunderstandings as listed above, one can best understand the martial arts by accurately analyzing such things as distance, geometry, and applying such concepts as resistance v non-resistance, effort v non-effort, and so on.

The result of understanding the Force/Flow matrix, and of correcting the various misunderstandings which result when various martial arts are analyzed, is that one begins to understand the Martial Arts from a more complete, call it 'holistic' if you will, viewpoint.

One must view the Martial Arts as a complete picture, and not a bunch of splintered and sometimes opposing concepts and theories.

Analysis of the Matrices you have seen thus far lead directly to the following sequence of maps.

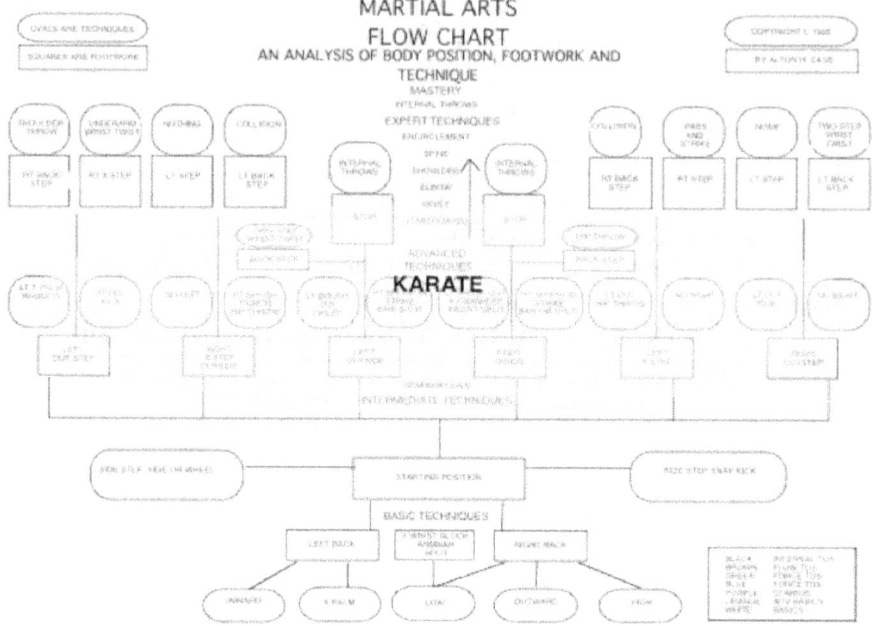

This is a flow chart for the art of Karate.

Yes, there will be anomalies, and these are the result of people attempting to absorb/insert techniques from other arts.

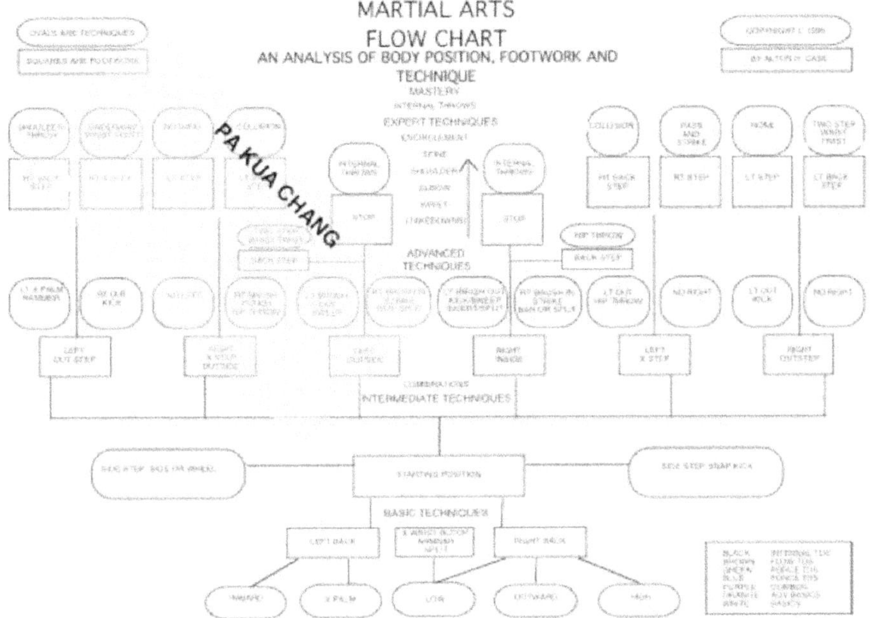

Here is Pa Kua Chang.

You will see, in these maps, that each art has a particular place on the overall map, and specific geometries of techniques, strategic formulations, and so on.

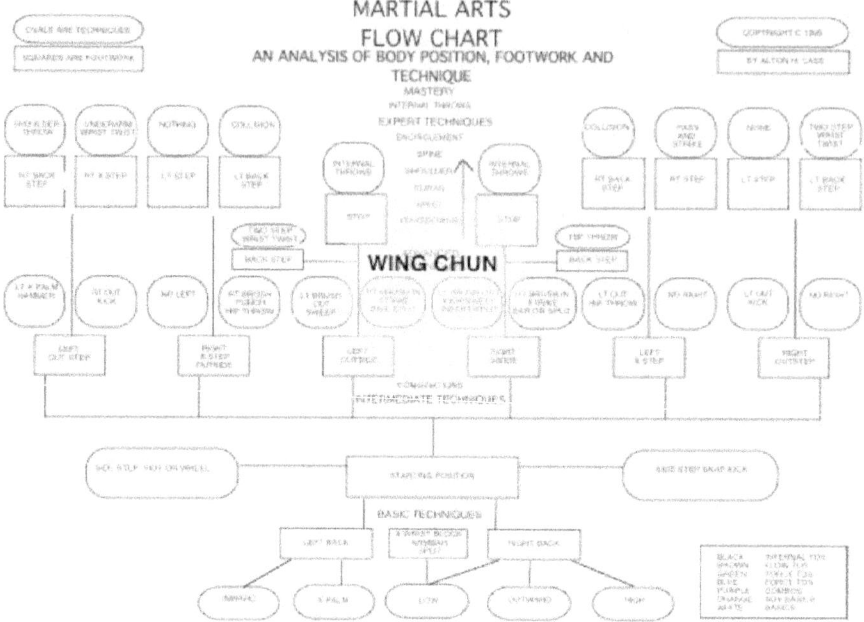

Don't misunderstand the maps and think a specific art is limited to a specific location or type of motion, for simple motion opens every art into an advantageous position which can handle ALL attacks.

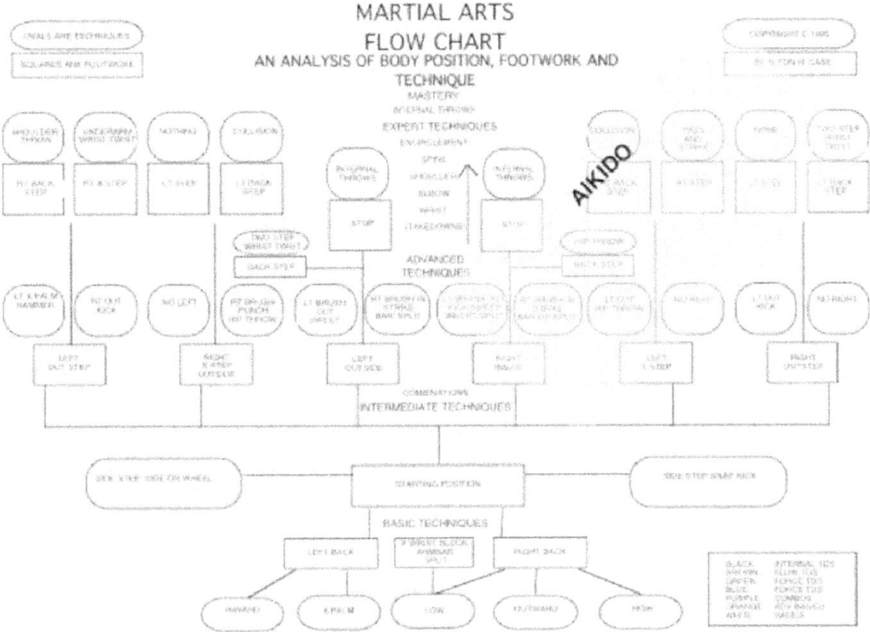

One fact to be taken away from this Flow Chart Analysis of the Martial Arts is that dedication to the point of zealousness can make anything work, and this has the added benefit of enabling an individual to plumb his depths, and to make anything work.

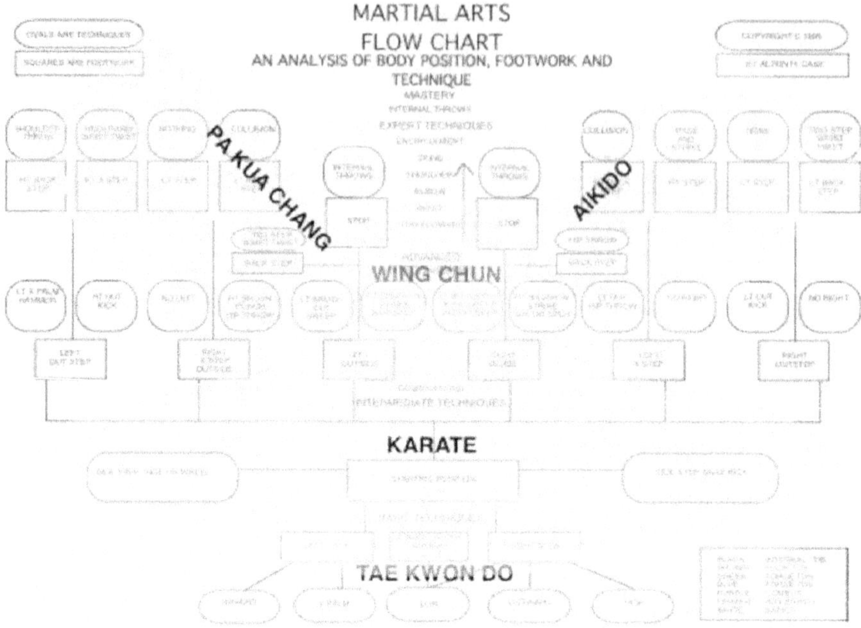

When one overlaps all maps, however, one can see that all art are one.

One can then understand that attempting a complete understanding of ALL arts would give far more depth than ANY single art.

And, it would be, in the end, a much faster study.

Much.

chapter nine
Finding the Basic-Basics

The Martial Arts, because the Arts are 'inbred,' and because human beings don't understand their inherent nature, are approached (taught) backwards.

All too often instructors dwell on the significance of techniques and forms, and neglect the basics.

Worse, all too few instructors actually understand the Basic-Basics underlying all martial arts.

This is one thing that study of the preceding matrices, and a few decades of intense practice, taught the author.

Breathing

The secret of life.

Breath out when the body expands, breath in when it contracts.

Breath out when you strike or are struck.

Breath as if to the tan tien (the one point), which is located an inch below the navel. Oxygen will descend to the diaphragm, then an energy wave will descend from the diaphragm to the one point. The tan tien is the energy center for the body, and energy will emit from the tan tien once you breath down to it.

Once you are actually producing energy you can begin to direct it throughout the body, and even outside of the body.

Relaxing

Energy travels best through what is relaxed; energy travels slower through what is tense.

Use the discipline of the Martial Arts to learn how to use intention to direct energy.

Grounding

Use breathing and relaxing to sink the weight of the body and thus make a better connection to the ground.

The actual formula here is: Weight = Work = Energy

You sink the weight, thus making the legs work harder. The more you work, the more energy you create.

This energy can be directed through the body and into your technique.

The 'secret' here is that the body is a motor, and that motors only work when they are connected to a base (bolted down, otherwise fixed in space). If the motor is not fixed in space the torque created by the motor will cause the motor to move, thus causing misalignment, loss of energy, and even destruction of the motor.

Observe the motor mounts of a car, other means of fixing a motor in space, even the tail prop of a helicopter.

Alignment

When the channels of a motor open (are relaxed), and energy is created by breathing, and the motor is fixed in space, one has to align the working parts of the motor.

Body alignment.

One can test the fixed alignment of the body by pressing on the fist, or working part of a martial arts technique, and observing the energy passing through the arm, down the body, down the legs, and into the ground.

The next step would be to have body alignment in motion, which is CBM, or Coordinated Body Motion.

CBM is when all parts of the body support one intention; when all parts of the body start motion at the same time, and cease motion at the same time.

Concepts

The last thing to be understood in this concept of basic basics, and this is not a Basic-Basic, but nevertheless must be understood, is that of concepts.

One can tailor the Basic-Basics to make Basics efficient, and to support the various concepts of the martial arts.

chapter ten
Matrixing Grounding

In the following matrices bear in mind that positive is weight going down the leg, negative is weight going up the leg.

Be aware that there are degrees of energy going up or down. Most two legged stances will have degrees of downward flow, and not a true upward flow for the negative leg.

Generally speaking, for most arts, you can sink energy down one leg, the other leg, both legs, or no legs.

Because there are two potentials here, one leg or two legs, we must draw two matrixes.

One Leg

	positive	negative
positive	crane stance	
negative		jumping

Only two squares are filled out here. That's what happens when you have two values (positive and negative) and one leg

Here's the second matrix.

Two Legs

	positive	negative
positive	horse stance	front stance
negative	back stance	jumping

So the complete list, from these two matrixes, would be this.

One leg	positive	crane stance
Two legs	positive/positive	horse stance
Two legs	positive/negative	front stance
Two legs	negative/positive	back stance
No legs	negative/negative	jumping

And, you could 'warp' this list by:

twisting stances (dragon stance)
lengthen the stances (snake stance)

And so on.

chapter eleven
Matrixing Alignment

There are four basic alignments.

Alignment refers to the connection from the earth to the fist (contact point).

The four basic alignments are

	right foot	**left foot**
right hand	right foot to right hand (lunging punch)	left foot to right hand (reverse punch)
left hand	right foot to left hand (reverse punch)	left foot to left hand (lunging punch)

Obviously there are going to be many more potential alignments.
BUT, there are (potential) problems with other alignments.
Consider the following short list for a horse stance.

horse stance to the right hand
horse stance to the left hand
horse stance to both hands
horse stance to no hands

Upon first consideration, one might say, 'Why not?'
As everyone knows, a horse stance with punches is a basic training drill!

But take a look at Chinese concepts and you will find a term called 'double weighting.'
It is an interesting term, and it refers to splitting your intention down both legs, which is weaker than dropping the intention down one leg.
Mind, I am not saying double weighting is right or wrong; one might consider this a stylistic difference.

Here is the argument concerning 'double weighting.':

If a person is dropping weight down both legs then he may lack balance when pushed from the front or back. He may have better balance when push from the side (able to run the opponent's energy sideways through his body to the ground).

But as a training drill designed to teach beginners how to sink the weight when punching, it works well.

So there are going to be plus and minus arguments (a regular matrix of arguments) when considering the value of the various alignments in stances.

Make a list for every stance you know. Combine those stances with punches and blocks.

Interestingly, you may find the lists becoming a bit lengthy. That's okay, just remember that matrixing was originally a compilation of lists until I found the 'truth table' that I currently use.

At the end of all the lists, at the end of the matrices, is complete understanding of the martial arts.

Read that again: COMPLETE UNDERSTANDING OF THE MARTIAL ARTS!

That is a goal worth seeking.

It is a goal that has eluded all, until the advent of matrixing.

So decide that you want complete understanding, then make the lists and matrices, and then get a friend and do all the potential techniques.

chapter twelve
Matrixing Punches

There are two types of punches: curved, and straight. These punches can be described in various ways, hook, jab, cross, uppercut, and so on.

Karate, classical karate, usually uses straight punches. This is because if you throw a punch with the shoulder it will twist the stance, but a straight punch feeds, and is fed by, the stance. The punch utilizes alignment to reach the ground.

This is not a statement of good or bad, merely a description of technique.

Regardless of whether you practice a classical form of karate, or one more aimed at fighting, or a different art or sport entirely, the two punches are curved or straight.

Here is a basic matrix for the potentials of these punches.

	curved	straight
curved	curved/curved	curved/straight
straight	straight/curved	straight/straight

This matrix describes all potential punch combinations.
Curved/curved would describe a pair of hooks.
Straight/straight might be a pair of jabs.
You should make a list of all the various punches and decide whether they are curved or straight, and then matrix them so as to understand the potentials (potential body alignments, etc.) encountered when putting together combinations.

It may seem to get a bit complex when you consider that you can punch with the right hand, or the left hand, in combination. But the reality, once matrixed, is fairly simple.

	right	left
right	right/right	right/left
left	left/right	left/left

Now you can see that punching with one hand only occurs at right/right or left/left, and punching with two hands only occurs at right/left and left/right.

Make a list of the four hand potentials (right or left), then list the curved or straight potentials underneath each of the rights and lefts and combinations.

Then explore these punches off the various stances with an eye to applying the matrix of alignments from the last chapter.

chapter thirteen
Matrixing Punches 2

There are two other types of punches: thrust and snap.

The thrust goes through, and the snap 'bounces' off (leaving impact in the target).

Here is the matrix.

	thrust	**snap**
thrust	thrust/thrust	thrust/snap
snap	snap/thrust	snap/snap

Which punch you use depends on a couple of things, whether you are small in stature, or large, whether you are quick on your feet, or slow, what the immediate situation is, and so on.

This factors can be understood by drawing simple matrices to explore them.

To understand the above matrix simply go back to earlier chapters and analyze the right/left factors, the body alignment factors, and so on.

chapter fourteen
Matrixing Blocks

In this chapter you will see the original matrix, Matrix Number One, if you will, the matrix that started it all.

I was making huge lists of potentials, grouping blocks with stances and changes of direction and so on, and the thing was unwieldy. I had lists that were literally thousands of items long, then art specific, and growing. I think at one time I visualized something like 256,000 potential techniques, should one isolate the elements of each technique.

Then, inspiration filtering into me from somewhere, I made this matrix.

	low	high	outward	inward
low	low/low	low/high	low/out	low/in
high	high/low	high/high	high/out	high/in
outward	out/low	out/high	out/out	out/in
inward	in/low	in/high	in/out	in/in

After this matrix I went forward, made more complex matrices, and backward, making the simpler matrices you have seen earlier in this book.

This was the acorn from which grew the oak. I began to create forms and sequences of techniques that represented ALL techniques.

But, I have to say, just knowing this matrix won't make you a master, only knowing the forms and techniques I created to represent the various matrices, and being able to do them, will make you a master.

But Matrixing actually started with this simple blocking matrix.

chapter fifteen
Matrixing Blocks 2

As stated in the last chapter, just knowing the blocking matrix won't make you a master.

But why does this particular matrix work so well?

Consider the following matrix.

	low	high	outward	inward
low	low/low (advanced var.)	low/high (version)		
high				
out				
in			out/out (advanced var.)	

In this matrix you will find the techniques presented in the form Pinan One (Heian One), which is one of the first forms in many classical karate systems.

Look at all the blank spots! 81% of the matrix (the form) is blank! And the remaining 19% are versions or variations!

So after learning the first four blocks of Karate the student is slanted off into blankness and deviation.

THERE IS NO LOGIC IN THIS!

There is no orderly presentation of forms, techniques, or even freestyle.

There is no science; the martial arts, in this case Karate, are collections of random motions.

All of which explains why Matrixing is so phenomenally successful.

Simply, people like viewing the art as a science; they like taking orderly steps to black belt.

Of course, this results in the death of mysticism, and most black belts came through the mystical approach, and so have a difficult time giving it up.

This is why you will sometimes hear martial artists decrying the matrix approach. Invariably, they have not studied matrixing, and are only making a knee jerk response to something that threatens to put order in the martial arts, and which takes the mystery out of the martial arts.

And, I will say at this time: when you do an art scientifically the mind reacts differently; the mind stops resisting having to jump gaps of knowledge, having to make sense out of that which doesn't make sense, and starts absorbing at a furious rate.

The mind becomes quick and intuitive.

The mind likes it.

The problem is that most students have a difficult time putting aside previous methods of learning.

The human being has been indoctrinated and tends to distrust learning.

Quite a thing to learn from a simple matrix. Eh?

chapter sixteen
Blank Spots

One thing I want to mention here, important enough to have its own chapter, in spite of there not even being a matrix in this chapter, is the fact of 'blank spots.'

Blank spots as revealed in the matrix of the last chapter.

When a person learns through the repetition of form method that is so prevalent, he will gain competence slowly. Slowly, because the mind is struggling to jump over the blank spots that occupy the form.

With a matrix there are no blank spots.

A person is as good at the martial arts, and even life, or as bad, in relation to the number of blank spots he has.

Blank spots in the form become blank spots in the mind.

The matrixing method includes not just the study of matrices, but the rearrangement of forms, techniques, and even freestyle, so that there are no blank spots. This is the reason a matrixed martial art can be learned 3 to 10 times faster.

chapter seventeen
Matrixing Blocks 3

Here's an advanced matrix of blocks.

Bear in mind that without the sequencing of techniques into logical forms it will merely be a curiosity.

That sequencing of techniques into simple forms is available on the Matrix Karate course.

	low	high	out	in	X hi	X low	palm	invert low
low								
high								
out								
in								
X low								
X high								
palm								
invert low								

The above matrix presents a complete art, an art which surrounds the body and accounts for every angle of attack and defense.

Note that there are 64 potential techniques.

This is a huge amount of material, and it took some thought to figure out how to teach it in simple form and in a sequence of logical techniques.

Further, this is only one representation of the material. One can change timing and make 192 techniques quite easily, as is revealed in the next chapter.

chapter eighteen
matrixing timing

Martial Arts material can be subdivided into separate sets of timing.

block then counter
block and counter (simultaneous)
counter first

	block then counter	block and counter	counter first
block then counter			
block and counter			
counter first			

Block then Counter means that you are reacting after the attack.
Block and Counter means you are acting with the attack.
Counter First means you are are acting before the attack.

There is a drill specifically aimed at this matrix, it is called 'High-Low.' I believe this drill is on the Outlaw Karate course.

chapter nineteen
Combining Matrixes

Combining matrixes is quite interesting, and will quickly lead one to the heart of the art.

BUT, you can't smush the matrixes. You can't make one matrix out of two concepts. You have to isolate the concept, matrix it in motion, and then do a second and different matrix to the results.

For instance, take the blocking matrix, which is 64 techniques.

Apply the timing matrix, and you will have 192 techniques.

Apply a simple right/left matrix (see below)…

right/right
right/left
left/right
left/left

…and you will have 768 techniques.

Then do a stance matrix, and kick punch matrix and a…can you see how complex it can get?

It gets so complex that people will study for a lifetime and create a magnificent complex martial arts system, and never realize that they have bypassed the simplicity presented by matrixing.

chapter twenty
Matrixing Limbs

Here's an interesting matrix.

	r arm	l arm	r leg	l leg
r arm				
l arm				
r leg				
l leg				

With this matrix you can export all the potential combinations of attack.

Further, you can expand the matrix to include other weapons.

Further, you can combine this with a matrix of high and low, or other subdivisions of places to attack.

The interesting thing is this:

Once you have understood, and done (to a certain extent) such a combination of matrices as I explain in this book, you gain a confidence.

There is simply nothing you don't know, there are no blank spots, and thus whenever an opponent moves you will see the blank spots in his defense, you will see the things he doesn't understand.

It will make you a master, maybe even make you virtually unbeatable.

Simply, you will not be working on coping with a moment with a mind filled with blank spots, but rather applying your vast knowledge, using your 'blank spotless' persona, to dissect and take apart your opponent's plethora of blank spots.

chapter twenty-one
A Cautionary About Making Things Complex

I have to give you some data here, lest you begin to think that matrixing is complex.

Matrixing can be complex, but you need to keep it simple.

Understand how to combine matrixes, play with it, but when things get too heavy, back off and return to the simplicities.

It is all too easy for the martial arts to get too large and complex, especially considering the material of the past few matrixes.

But you don't have to get complex if you simply do the simple ones already presented, and are cautious of matrices that are too large and complex.

Although, to be sure, I encourage you to make a few complex matrices and explore for yourself, if only to find out that I am right.

The thing to remember is this:

You make a sequence of punches based on three.

right/right/right
right/right/left
right/left/right
right/left/left
left/right/right
left/right/left
left/left/right
left/left/left

It's a good matrix, you could even make an art around it.

Except every combination in the above list(matrix) is covered by this matrix.

right/right
right/left
left/right
left/left

So why make a complex matrix when the simple one already has all the moves?

But don't believe me. Try it for yourself.

You might find a couple of interesting things, you might even find that you think I am wrong.

Excellent.

Every person has to find out what is true for himself/herself.

chapter twenty-two
The Other Half of the Equation

It's not all about constructing the body for attack, you see, that is only half the equation.

There must be a yin to the yang, or a yang to the yin.

Or, as I like to say, for something to be true the opposite must also be true.

You can't understand attack unless you understand defense.

So, thus far, we have talking about constructing the body to attack.

But there must be a matrix for defense, there must be simple ways to construct the body to handle all that incoming force and flow.

Remember this concept, and consider it as we develop matrixing through to actual fighting.

chapter twenty-three
Six Distances

There are SEVEN distances to be considered.

Weapons (knife, gun, etc.)
Kicking
Punching
Kneeing
Elbowing
Takedowns
Grappling

Weapons would require individual matrices.
Here is a simple matrix for the striking range.

	kick	punch	knee	elbow
kick				
punch				
knee				
elbow				

Thus, one needs to learn how to kick twice, kick then punch, kick then knee, kick then elbow, and so on.

This can get confusing when you apply a right/left matrix to it. Better to just do this matrix with:

right/right
then right/left
then left/right
then left/left.

Apply this matrix to air strikes, bag strikes, static positions (holding kicks against walls, etc.) and so on.

(A matrix of resistances.)

Learn the distance of your strikes so that you have no weakness, so that you have no blank spot in your striking.

One thing you should know is this: time is distance. Thus, the opposite being true, distance is time.

Thus, you need to explore how time changes as you go through this matrix.

The reason this is important is because of this concept:

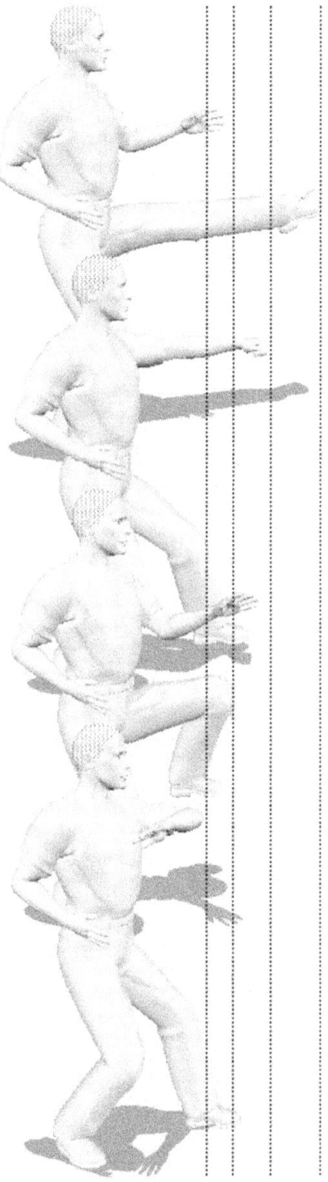

see/think/react

see/react

react

act

This is a matrix in list form; it describes the evolution of the person learning the martial arts. It describes how one shortens reaction time until there is no time; until one sees what is happening before it happens.

This is important because if one takes the mystical approach, if one refuses the logic of matrixing, then one is locked into body reaction time, and one will always have the potential of making mistakes.

But, if one approaches the art as a science, if one develops himself through each stage from seeing to acting, then one can master time and know when an opponent is going to attack before the attack; at the inception of the thought behind the attack.

chapter twenty-four
Three Stages of a Fight

Once one has realized the potential distances of his body, and knows the ranges of his body, he should become aware of the three stages of a fight.

The three stages of a fight are:

entering the fight
closing the distance
finishing the fight

Entering is when you can kick or punch.

Closing the distance is traveling through the knee and elbow distances.

Finishing the fight can be takedowns.

	enter	close	finish
enter			
close			
finish			

Obviously, there is going to be some mix and match here, and you will find some stark anomalies.

Takedowns can lead to grappling, which entails an entirely different matrix.

The real key to understanding the above matrix is being able to shift from one distance to another. Here is a list to help in this understanding.

Nine Potentials for Shifting Distance

Moving from entering to entering means the fight didn't fully engage, distance occurred, the fight has to be entered again. This is wasteful and dangerous. Every time you have a false start, or an incomplete entry to a fight, the opponent can analyze you.

Moving from Entering to Closing is a mere factor of distance. The trick is to be able to go from kicks and punches to knees and elbows. Or, to be able to trap and slip as you decrease distance.

Moving from entering to finishing could be a kick to a grapple. Not quite efficient, there are missed opportunities, and potential blank spaces. And, it could be a punch that knocks somebody out; that would be a successful entry to finish.

Moving from Closing to Entering is a tactic when the opponent is better at the mid range than you are, you can't find a way into the finish.

Closing to closing is merely a rearrangement of the mid-range distance. Maybe you are shifting sides, maybe you are changing the hand pattern, maybe you are stuck in mud.

Closing to finishing is slipping through the mid range into a takedown, or executing a strike that incapacitates.

Finishing to entering means your takedown, or fight ending strike failed, and you need to back up and reset.

Finishing to closing means the same things as the last sentence, except you are not going back so far. You are not going back to a reset, but merely back into the closing distance. This means you haven't totally messed up your takedown, maybe it sort of worked, but you aren't threatened enough by 'failure' to need to get the heck out of Dodge.

Finishing to finishing means you are doing a couple of takedowns, you are takedown into grappling, hitting him hard enough to knock him out twice, and so on.

The point: the person who controls distance controls the fight.

By understanding this matrix, by being able to shift from any range to any range (knowing your weapons well enough so that you can do this), you can control the fight QUITE effectively.

There are variations of this concept in various arts. Make sure you understand the purpose and intent of each range in whatever method you are using.

chapter twenty-five
Three Types of Fighters

There are three types of fighters. This concept, I believe, was first espoused by Traceys, who, I believe, learned it from Joe Lewis, who, I believe, learned it from Bruce Lee. Bruce Lee may have learned it in Wing Chun, or one of the other 26 arts he studied.

At any rate, it is a known theory with a few variations.

The three types of fighters are:

charger (one who is constantly attacking)
blocker (one who stands his ground and blocks and counters)
runner (one who is constantly retreating)

Here is the Matrix:

	charger	blocker	runner
charger			
blocker			
runner			

And, here is the list of potentials when two people fight.

Both are chargers. They clash and clash, and there is a lot of 'garbage.'

One is a charger and one is a blocker. The outcome depends on who is better.

One is a charger and one is a runner. An interesting contest of can somebody attack quick enough to not make a mistake…and the opposite is true.

Blocker and charger. See above.

Blocker and blocker. A contest of wits, of technique. Interesting, but not necessarily flashy.

Blocker and runner. A contest of frustration. Can the blocker sucker the runner in? Can the runner make the blocker charge?

Runner and charger. See above.

Runner and blocker. See above.

Runner and runner. It's like watching two people with leprosy play tag.

Who wins, in the above scenario, depends on which person is better. This is difficult to assess, as it is often like comparing apples to oranges.

BUT, I would say that ultimately the winner is going to be the person with the best technique, which would favor the blocker. But don't bet on it. Too many variables in the mix when you consider a human being, and especially against another human being.

The real truth here is that you must understand your strengths and weaknesses, you must be able to accurately assess yourself, and you must train so that you can't be labeled one kind of a fighter over another.

You must be able to adapt to any type of fighter by becoming the type of fighter which who can overcome the attributes of any type of fighter.

If the other person is a stronger type of fighter, you must be able to select the type of fighter, you must be able to change your mode of fighting, so that your strengths prevail.

Make sure that you play both roles when exploring the various situations.

chapter twenty-six
Three Types of Motion

Continuing in the vein of the last chapter, we need to consider the type of motion each type of fighter brings to a confrontation.

This is a very important consideration and ability. Understanding how motion really works you will be able to become any of the three types of fighters, and you will be well equipped when we enter more advanced concepts and matrices in the latter portions of this book.

You can go forward, hold your ground, or go back.

	go forward	harmony	go back
go forward			
harmony			
go back			

You may wonder at the inclusion of the term 'harmony' in the above matrix.

After all, shouldn't this term be 'like' blocking?

Initially, yes, but here's an interesting fact.

A fight is the collapsation of distance; when distance collapses there is a fight.

Think about it. The most insane, violent person, if put all by himself...WITH LOTS OF SPACE AROUND HIM...tends to relax.

Think about it. When somebody shoves somebody else's chest, the (potential) fight 'may' be defused by simply stepping back.

And, here is a very interesting fact: Harmony results from the maintaining of a distance.

This depends to a certain extent upon the distance being a non-threatening distance. Or the receiver of the threat being VERY good at harmonious methods of fighting. Read Aikido, Tai Chi, etc.

Here is how you make it work.

When a person steps angrily forward, you step with him, in the same direction, and talk soothingly.

When a person steps angrily away, you step with him, in the same direction, and talk soothingly.

Of course the person seeking harmony must be of sufficient intelligence that he can cope with the mental problems, with the emotional output, of the angry person. This mental ability can result from a study of harmonious martial arts.

There are other options, MANY options, but they start with this simplicity.

DON'T underestimate this strategy. It is supreme, once you have understood and can make it work.

You can make it work with any art if you have the ability to control distance and can bring someone into 'orbit' with yourself.

The trick is to first be able to control, and eliminate, your own anger.

This ability, of controlling your own anger, will become easier to understand as we proceed with our matrices.

It is easy to control anger when there are no blank spots.

chapter twenty-seven
Understanding the Body

To learn the martial arts, and to entertain hopes of mastering the martial arts, one must understand the body.

This means you must understand what motions a joint is capable of, and what muscles you must use to activate that joint.

For instance:
An elbow is a hinge.
What are the muscles above the elbow?
What are the muscles below the elbow?
How does each muscle make the elbow work?

This is a simple process, but you have to do it for every single joint in the body.

This entails knowledge of the joints in the body, the bones on each side of the joint, and the muscles attached to those bones which pull the bones to make the joint open or close.

And, there are a variety of joints in the body. There are joint that hinge, that are ball and socket, that slide, and so forth.

chapter twenty-eight
Understanding the Body 2

I have stated previously that the body has to perform some circular movements to attain straight motions.

From the other side of the equation, one has to understand how to circle each joint.

	right clockwise	right counter-clockwise	left clockwise	left counter-clockwise
wrist				
elbow				
shoulder				
neck				
spine				
hip				
knee				
ankle				

Simply circle each joint right or left, clockwise or counter clockwise, and you will find all useful grab arts.

Yes, there are a couple of tricks here, and even a couple of anomalies, but it is a simple process of analyzing how the human body works.

chapter twenty-nine
Karate Potentials of Motion

There are many different methods for summing up the potential motions of the body.

The geometry describing potentials of motion in karate is very often the square.

Consider the forms, most of the turns follow one or the other corners of a square: 90, 180, 270 degrees.

The initial blocks are the low, high, outward and inward, which describe up, down, left or right. The walls of a square.

Yes, there are arcs and different angles, but karate, especially classical karate, tends to hang on to the basic square through much of its development.

At any rate, it is easier to understand karate by analyzing with the square in mind, then taking note of other motions as you progress.

Following is a sample illustration of the square.

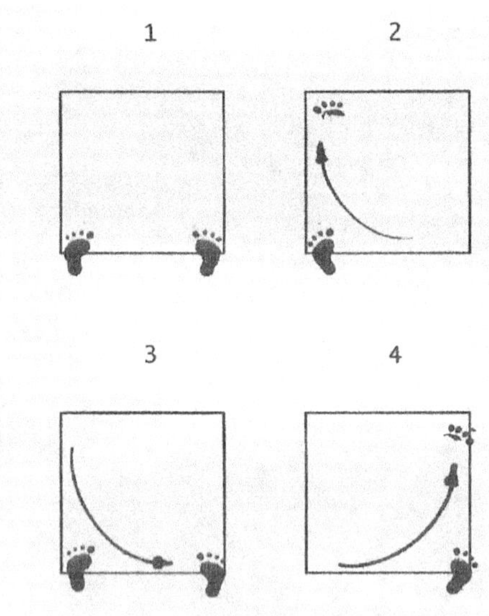

chapter thirty
More Potentials of Motion

My initial research on potentials of motion included a cube. This accounted for six directions: up, down, right, left, forward, back.

This would develop into the Nine Square Pattern, which you will see in a moment.

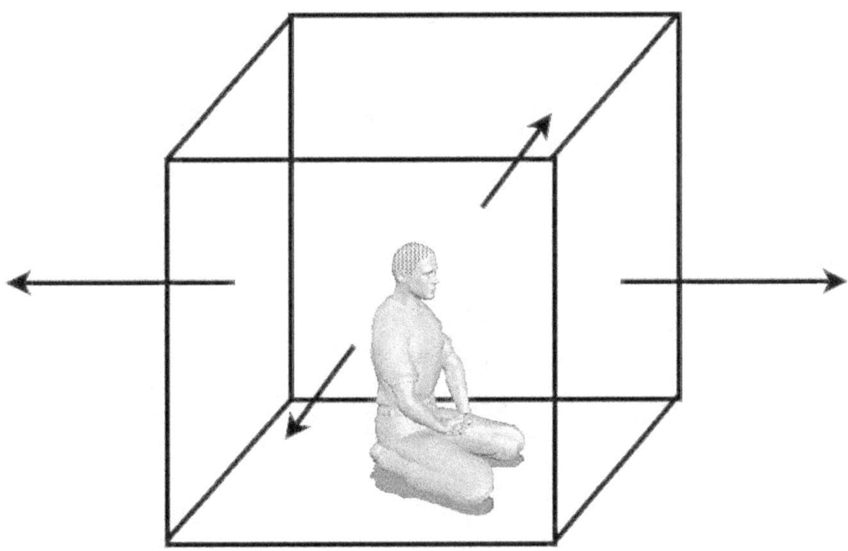

The point here is that one can move in any of the six directions, with certain conditions applied. Gravity, for instance, or the height of a jump.

I was very inspired by the Japanese saying: sit squarely in the room.

This saying encourages one to be aware of all the space in a room. Even if one is sitting in a corner of a room he can be aware of all the corners, all the planes describing walls, floors and ceiling, and all potentials of motion.

chapter thirty-one
Wing Chun Potentials of Motion

The potentials of motion in this chapter are described quite adequately in the book 'Wing Chun Kung Fu,' by James Yim Lee. James was one of Bruce Lee's students, and some say this book was authored (perhaps inspected in a most detailed manner, inspired, etc?) by Bruce.

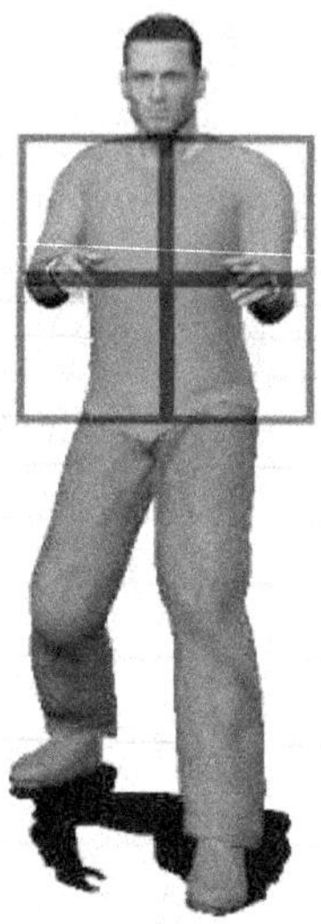

'Four Doors' for each hand
make the 'Eight Gates.'

The potentials of motion are based on a fixed, central elbow position.

From the 'elbowic' position the arms describe these motions, which are labeled 'doors:'

up to the right
up to the left
down to the right
down to the left

This visualization of the space in front of the body, the space 'traveled through' by an attacking limb, is quite ingenious.

Further, when one accounts for both hands one has 'eight gates,' and a complete fighting system with amazing depth and potential.

chapter thirty-two
Pa Kua Potentials of Motion

Pa Kua Chang (eight trigrams palm maneuvers) utilizes eight directions. These are the directions of the compass.

north
north west
west
south west
south
south east
east
north east

Interesting, the directions are accounted for with their specific emblem, the 8 trigrams symbol, and they do present many other potentials of motion.

The hands, however, circle and spiral.

circle right
circle left
spiral right
spiral left

Put together with the 'circle walking' method of of PKC, the system is quite complete and unique. One simply draws a matrix for the directions/changes on the circle and the circling/spiraling of the hands.

A note: towards the beginning of this tome I presented several 'maps. PKC and Aikido occupied two distinct portions of this map, and seem to be the right side and the left side of the map, duplicates in reverse.

This is sometimes accounted for, in some part, by the tendency of Aikido to utilize an 'open step,' and PKC to utilize a 'closed' (or cross) step.

It is interesting to note how many arts are similar, and in so many ways. One could do quite an analysis by using such mathematic terms as 'transversal,' 'reflect,' and so on.

chapter thirty-three
Nine Square Potentials of Motion

The six potentials of motion (a cube) described earlier easily evolve into nine squares.

First, after considering the method of dividing the body into zones utilized by Wing Chun, I divided the body into nines areas of attack.

One can visualize attacks to the various squares of the body.

This is similar to the eight angles of attack and defense presented by various Escrima arts.

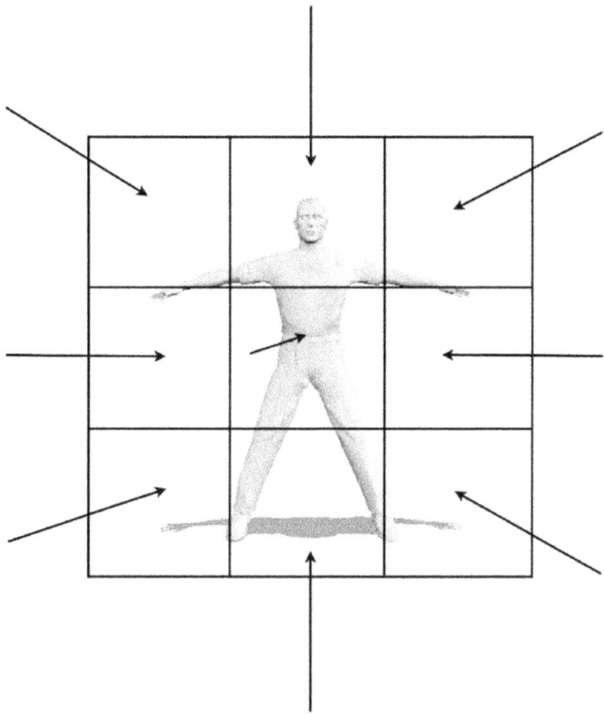

I also laid this pattern on the floor, which the idea that one could step into any square in avoiding an attack or working a technique.

One simply resets the pattern on the floor in the mind whenever a step is taken, which results in a brand new potential of motion in nine 'directions.'

chapter thirty-four
The Evolution of Potentials of Motion

Looking at the martial arts through the eyes of the various geometries brought me to an awareness of how the martial arts evolved.

2 ~ a yin yang
4 ~ a square
6 ~ a cube
8 ~ compass directions
And so on.

Here are a couple of the illustrations resulting from these cogitations.

The illustration on the right is a simple matrix exploring potential motions on a line.

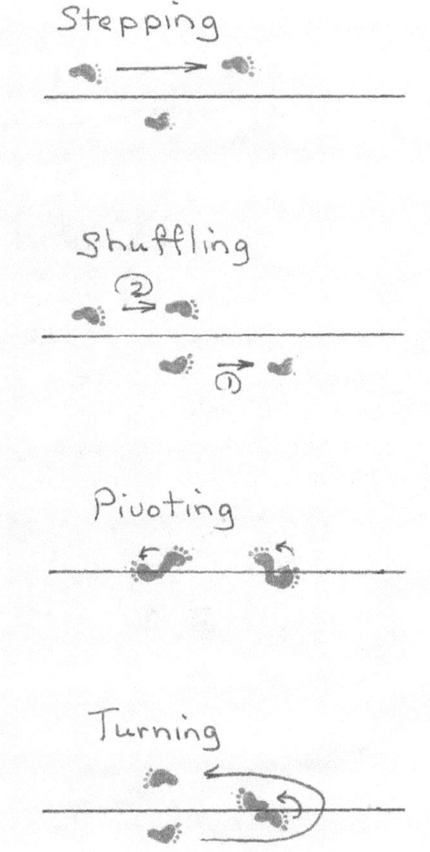

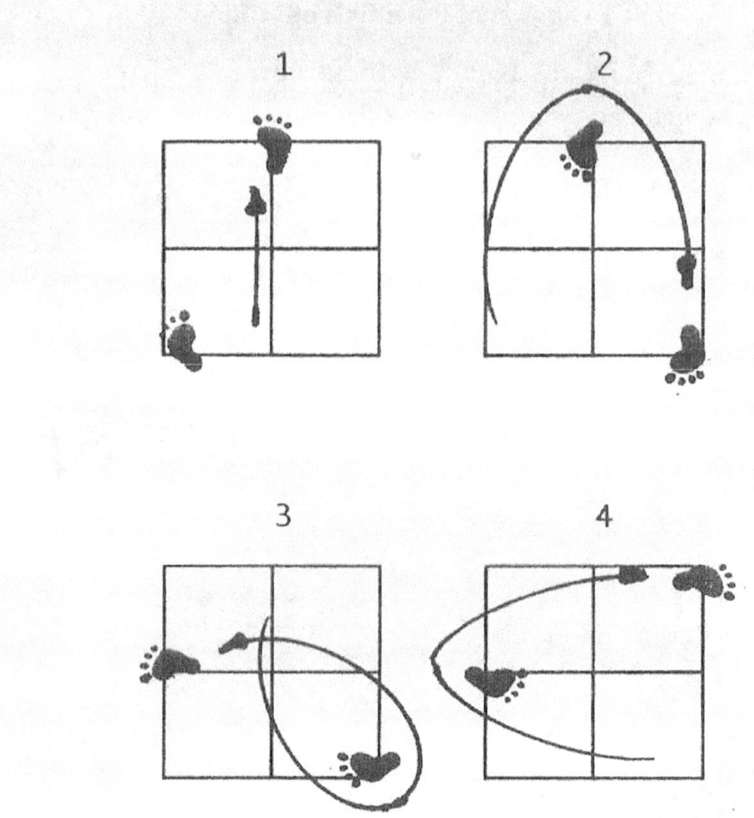

The above is an interesting variation based on four squares. There are four more steps, but they are easy to figure out, just continue the pattern presented by the first four steps.

I wore out a couple pair of shoes working through this one. The pivot just tore the bottoms up.

chapter thirty-five
Potentials of Motion for the Samurai Sword

One very interesting matrix I came up with involved the directions of the sword.

I was doing training drills called 'suburito.' I had developed this Japanese sword drill through various potentials of motion using the evolution of geometry I previously described.

I began to think about the foot work, about turning to face in any direction, and came up with the following matrix.

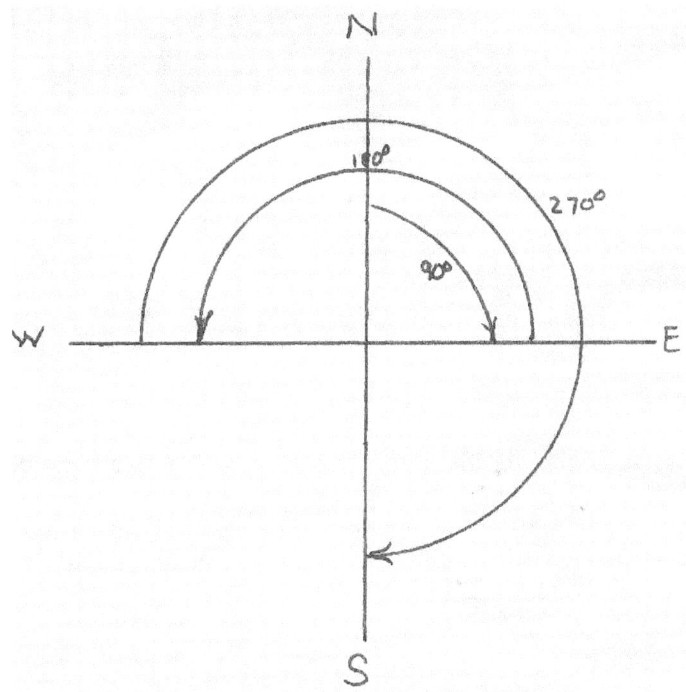

One can pivot to face any direction. This includes the three angles of 90 degrees, 180 degrees, and 270 degrees, and both clockwise and counter clockwise.

Put together with the footwork of the line, which I presented earlier, you have a complete description of basic (and some advanced) sword theory and techniques.

chapter thirty-six
The Directions of the Mind

After many years I became aware that there is thought before action.

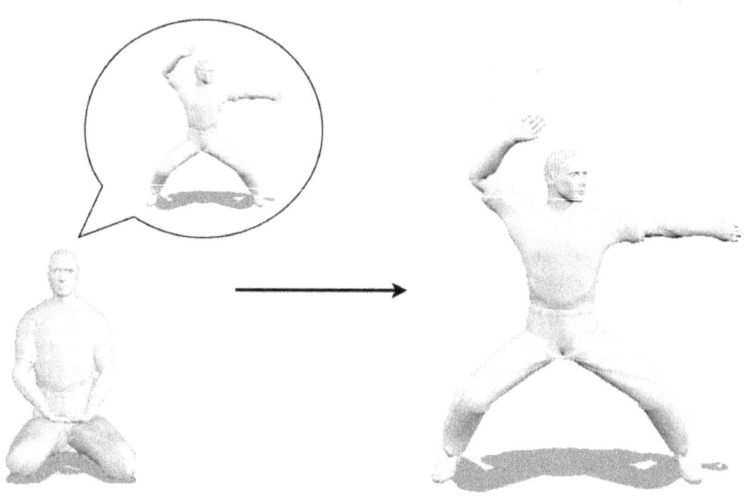

Above is a representation of a person having a thought before he does an action.

As time progresses, as one delves deeper and deeper into the art, one becomes aware of, can actually perceive, a person having a thought before an action.

One can actually see the thought before the action. This is the truth: there MUST be a thought before an action, there can be no action without a preceding thought.

One of the things a martial artist tries to do is have action at the same time as a thought. One continually perceives space between the inception of a thought and the resulting action; one is constantly attempting to shorten this distance between thought and action until it happens at the same time.

And it is possible, but it requires delving into some VERY advanced martial arts concepts, and some VERY intense practice.

chapter thirty-seven
The Emotional Directions of the Mind

To find perfection, which is the same as eliminating the distance between thought and action, one must deal with emotions.

It is usually assumed that one must have no emotions.

This is one of the most misunderstood concepts in the martial arts, and in life.

One can have happiness, and other such emotions.

One shouldn't have such emotions as anger, fear, and so on.

Happiness manifests outwards.

Anger goes inward.

Yes, emotions go both ways, but when one has destructive emotions he is destroying those around himself, and driving himself further and further into a pit of despair.

Happy emotions strengthen one, and lift up those around him, and make life better.

But this is mere descriptive icing. Everybody knows that what goes around comes around, that there is 'karma,' and that in any number of cultural observations and descriptions.

To get to the truth of handling emotion we have to consider what, EXACTLY, emotion is.

Did you know that nobody knows what emotion actually is?

To my knowledge NOBODY has ever defined emotion.

There's schools of thought on handling emotion, handling the emotion of other people, but nobody has ever defined EXACTLY what emotion is.

Emotion is motion in the mind. It is generated by the spiritual being. It is a form of communication, sometimes on a level with animal manifestations, and sometimes a manifestation of sublimity.

A human being controls his destiny, controls his life, and he manifests happy emotions. He shares with the world, generating 'vibrations' of emotion which show his success and happiness.

Or, a human being is out of control, and he manifests such things as pain, anger, fear. He shares with the world, generating these 'vibrations' of emotions.

It is a deeper level of communication than words, a more honest level of communication.

It is motion in the spirit (or the mind), and the mind, like a good radio transmitter, shares these emotions with any and everybody within 'hearing.'

chapter thirty-eight
The Directions of the Human Being

In the beginning, everything is simple. A person is one, a spiritual being, an awareness.

During the process of life he seeks active knowledge and ability of himself.

He is stymied by confusion, distraction, all manner of misdirection.

Consider the following list.

body
mind
emotion
fantasy
spirit

This is the path that one must take to find the truth of themselves through the martial arts.

The martial arts are a discipline which enable the human being to control himself on all levels.

One must control his body; he must control (ignore) his mind; the mind is just a bunch of memories, so you ignore that.

One must stop being a 'radio station' for the level of communication that is emotion. One must control the motion inside their head to do this.

This does not include emotions of happiness, which are beneficial to all.

Finally, one must control such things as wishes and desires, dreams and fantasies, so that one's thought is pure; so that one is pure as a spirit, as an awareness.

In the end, one is attempting to return to simply being aware.

chapter thirty-nine
How to Control Emotion

How does one actually control emotion?
Consider this matrix.

	motion	emotion
motion		
emotion		

Motion to motion is the act of fighting with the bodies.

BUT, there is a sub-level, or perhaps 'over-level,' which is emotion and body.

Emotion to emotion is simply radiating emotions at one another without physicality.

What this means is that when somebody is coming towards you, you have to deal with two items: motion AND emotion.

Simple illustrations of this:

Angry man coming towards you with a knife.
Angry man coming towards you with flowers.

You need to avoid the man with the knife.
But, what do you do with the man with the flowers?

There is a mix of emotions with the man with the flowers. Is he angry at you? Is he angry with somebody else? Is he going to beat you to death with the flowers?

And, another illustration.

A woman crying while going away with a gun.

A woman crying while going away without a gun.

What? Why?

And the problem is this: do you remember when I told you that you had to be careful when combining matrices? In these problems, which include BOTH motion and emotion, you might have to apply two matrices: one for motion, (is it towards or away), and one for emotion, (is it good for you or bad for you.

People get confused, really confused, when motion is confused by emotion (motion inside the head) which is being broadcast at them.

A fighter who is angry can actually slow down motions with his emotions. Both your motion and his.

A fighter who is fearful can be coming towards you with motion while going away with motion inside his head. This gives you a confusion of signals, which gives you a confusion which must be penetrated before you can solve the problem(s).

When you have a person who is manifesting a single direction with both motion and emotion he is relatively easy to figure out.

When you have a person who is manifesting two directions, one away and one towards, it is much harder to figure out…and weird things can happen.

Consider this matrix:

	motion coming towards	motion going away
emotion coming towards		
emotion going away		

Motion and emotion coming towards is fairly easy to understand. There is a single direction, and it is easy to discern whether it is going to be destructive or beneficial.

Motion and emotion going away is likewise easy to understand; beneficial or destructive, going away is no threat.

BUT, motion and emotion going in different directions, one away and one towards, is a mixed signal and difficult to analyze.

So, what is the solution here?

First, the motion: go towards or away, depending on which direction will increase harmony.

Second, the emotion: go towards or away, depending on which direction will increase harmony.

Two solutions which may, or may not be, simple. In the matrix below the inner boxes are solutions based on the input of motion and emotion. Motion is reversed, as is emotion.

	motion coming towards	motion going away
emotion coming towards	motion away/ emotion away	motion towards/ emotion away
emotion going away	motion away/ emotion going towards	motion towards/ emotion towards

These are potential solutions. They depend on how extreme the motions are (running towards you? Sauntering towards you?) And what the exact motion is.

Beware, there is MUCH trickery here.

Would running after a man with a gun (he is going away) be correct?

Would you run towards a person who was crying? Wouldn't that scare him/her off?

Would a better solution involve a different motions and emotions?

These are very difficult questions; questions which require a profound knowledge of the implications of motion, AND a profound knowledge of the implications of emotion.

What you need to do now is make a list of emotions, then make another list of the same emotions right next to it.

Take the first emotion and compare it to each emotion on the second list. Find out which emotion seems to be the most likely to work.

Observe emotions in people, try out the results of your combing lists.

Doesn't work? Find more emotions. Find more solutions.

This is VERY creative work.

The last thing I want to re-emphasize: don't confuse motion with emotion.

Differentiate what the person is doing 'motionally' from emotionally. Don't confuse what he is doing with his body with what he is doing in his head.

Don't get confused with an emotion that may seem to be coming towards you and assign it to a motion.

There are two layers here: motion and emotion. You must matrix both of them, in separate matrices, and you must see them for what they are and separate them so you can choose the best solution(s).

Guaranteed, when you achieved a bit of martial discipline, and applied it to understanding the differences between motion and emotion, and have practiced handling motion and emotion through the simple application of creating motions that are counter and aimed towards creating harmony, you will have controlled the emotion in your mind.

You will be a simple person with an honest soul, and you will be more happy than you ever imagined.

chapter forty
The Directions of Fantasy

As you rid yourself of distractions to your martial arts, and achieve a single direction to your motion in life…

As you rid yourself of emotions through understanding and differentiating and handling emotions…

…you become a more pure, simpler kind of person.

You become you.

Undistracted, undivided, singular of intention.

Your danger then is not to betray yourself through your fantasies.

If you quell and ignore fantasies that are destructive, and this includes dreams of, plans for, and so forth, in directions that are less than constructive, then you grow as a spirit. You become more aware, spread more happiness, make life better and better for a larger and larger pool of humanity.

If you give in to fantasies that are destructive; if you do things in life that don't grow you (and humanity) as a spirit; if you don't stop hindering the growth of yourself, then you will shrink, become less and less aware.

The arena of life will become smaller and smaller, and the size and quantity of your defeats will grow ever larger.

If you quell and ignore plans for life that benefit all, then you become smaller.

If you give in to fantasies, which means purposes and plans and goals and all manner of things which benefit human kind, then you grow larger and larger, and there IS no limit to your growth.

The scale revealed by matrixing and the discipline of the martial arts looks like this:

Create beneficial fantasies ~ more awareness
Ignore destructive fantasies ~ potential for awareness
Ignore beneficial fantasies ~ dwindling awareness
Create destructive fantasies ~ less awareness

Obviously, one can align such things as the degree of your happiness, or unhappiness, with this list.

The question is simple, as are the answers.

Do you want to be good and realize the benefits of goodness?

Or do you want to be destructive and miss out on the benefits of goodness, and create a life of misery?

Matrixing, for all the matrices I have shown you here, for all the complexities and distractions you have to deal with, is simple.

The choice is simple.

Even the path is simple, once you decide to walk it.

Good or bad.

Positive or negative.

Plus or minus.

It IS a binary universe, and the solution is to seek, through good decisions, the singularity of yourself.

conclusion

Matrixing IS the science of the martial arts.

Matrixing was discovered by myself, and this includes not just the matrices I have listed here, but a large quantity of forms, techniques, drills, exercises, and more.

Matrixing can be applied, and should be applied to other fields.

It is, after all, a logic that can be applied to the areas of life with simplicity, thus changing life into a simple laboratory, instead of a confusing sequence of destructive distractions.

I have applied matrixing not only to the martial arts, but to such fields as language, mathematics, religion, and so on.

Binary Matrixing in the Martial Arts

The First and Only Science of the Martial Arts

or,
How to Grow the Martial Arts from the ground Up

or,
The Scientific Way to Enlightenment in the Martial Arts

Table of Contents for Binary Matrixing

introduction

Welcome!

Good to see you.

Pretty nifty title, eh?

Well, it's true.

I am going to introduce you to the first and only science of the martial arts, which is called matrixing. It is a form of logic that results in clarified thinking and better martial arts.

And, I am going to show you how to grow a martial art, the true martial art, from the ground up.

And, the result of this scientific analysis of how to grow the true martial art from the ground up is going to cause your enlightenment.

All you have to do is read this book, and do it.

The fact is that this is a whammer slammer of a book that takes no prisoners, leaves no doubt, and cannot be refuted.

After you finish this book you will see how a martial art is grown.

In fact, you will see, by matrixing, how the martial arts came to evolve, and what they are. What the truth of them is.

And you will know that I am telling the truth when I write things describing the various courses, things like:

'learn ten times faster,'
'find out all the things you didn't know,'
'understand the martial arts better than the old masters.'

At heart, I am hoping that you will slap your head, open your wallet, and take advantage of this vast body of wisdom that I am offering; that you will avail yourself of the matrixing courses on MonsterMartialArts.com.

But it's okay if you don't.

Look, there is a painting in a museum. Not everybody likes it. Some people will argue about it, some people will praise it. But not everybody will like it.

So if it is not for you, if you object to my scientific rendering of the arts, that's okay.

The world is big and wide and there is plenty of room for people and they can think whatever they want and that certainly is okay with me.

But if you do see truth in what I say here, then great!
Welcome home, brother.

There are several chapters of theory here. If you're not into theory, sorry, but it is crucial, and if you don't get what I am saying here this system isn't going to mean much to you. Your enlightenment is in serious doubt.

So read the theory. Take your time and figure it out, it is really going to pay off in the end.

After all, this is drastically different stuff you're going to be doing, and the theory is quite a bit different than anything you have ever read.

Okay?
Let's go.

Chapter One
The Universe

This universe is nothing but objects that flow. Every atom, every cell, every combination of molecules that make up an object, be it an ant or a sun, has a path.

Where the paths collide we have force.

Slow force, fast force…where objects collide there is force.

Thus, the universe is built on force and flow.

When you have existence in this universe you are trying to make sure that no bad collisions happen to you; that only good collisions happen to you.

Simply, the paths you take intersect the paths of others, and you have life.

Chapter Two
The Question

Before we get going on the martial arts I need to ask you something: I need to ask you about the kind of person you are: I need to know why you do, or wish to do, the Martial Arts.

Our paths are intersecting, and I need to ask you this question so that the intersection is pleasant, and not a violent and painful collision.

So why do you do the martial arts?

And, while you're thinking about this, let me say that the martial arts are a fantasy. That is a truth of the martial arts.

Think about it: out of all the people who go to dojos and practice, who sweat in their backyards, who buy books and videos and watch the movies and all that...how many of them have killed somebody?

So why do you do the martial arts?

You practice techniques to maim, to kill, but most of these techniques won't work in the octagon. They won't even work on the street!

But you practice, and you practice...so what do you get out of it all?

And, that question asked. let's get down to the nitty gritty: why do you practice the martial arts?

To make sure you understand where I am going, and that you will actually GET the enlightenment I offer you in this course, I need you to understand why you do martial arts.

While this bit of information worms through you, has its effect, let's return to the question: why do you study the martial arts?

Is it because you have been fantasizing? That's okay. If you can see that, if you can recognize the bogus nature of it all, then you are ready for a matrixing course.

If you are not, then the good news is that a matrixing course will likely get you there, but even if it doesn't, just keep practicing. You WILL experience space, and you WILL see each and every unique thought behind each and every unique action in this universe. And you will get there.

Have you been studying the martial arts for self defense?

That's fine. But know that once you are integrated, complete (not subject to the collision of multiple thoughts in your head), enlightened, and have a clue, you won't be.

You will likely stop generating the kinds of thoughts that bring you to fighting. After all, if you ask yourself what kind of thought you generated every time you get in a fight, shortly you will stop generating those thoughts. Not a guarantee, but a likelihood for 99% of the people who take a matrixing course.

And now you have to ask yourself, now that you have been stripped of fantasy and self defense: why are you studying the martial arts?

Have you been studying the martial arts to beat up people? To dominate them? To…insult them? You're in the wrong place. Good thing I caught you before you spent any money. Simply, your evil purposes will not survive this course, so you'd better pop on out of here right now.

And if you are studying the martial arts to beat somebody in the ring…ooops.

You aren't studying a martial art. You are studying a sport.

Nothing wrong with that, but you might, again, be in the wrong place.

In a sport you fight others.

In an art you fight yourself…to find the truth of yourself. I know, sounds a bit 'zen-ish,' but it's true. You are fighting to divest yourself of those distractions that keep you from discovering the truth of yourself.

At any rate, you can continue with this course if you wish, but to get the true benefit you will have to give up beating people up, and start fighting your way to the truth of yourself.

So, why are you studying the martial arts?

Not to defend, not to fantasize, not to beat people up…what's left?

Health? A better body?

How about friends and good times?

How about…to be a better human being.

If, in some regard, you have phrased this in your mind, even if it lurks behind the facade of what you don't know, then you are in the right place.

But, whatever the reason you come up with, it is yours, and you should consider this question until you have a reason that works, that will work beyond a career, or marriage, or any of the distractions of life.

A reason that you will take to the grave.

Indeed, a reason that will take you to the grave, for life will not seem complete unless you have and live by that reason.

It is your life, your reason, and I can't tell you why.

I can, however, tell you my why. The reason why I study the martial arts. There's no harm in that.

My reason for studying the martial arts is that I can't stop. I can't stop thinking about them. I can't stop working out. I can't stop, even if I am working with the fantasy arts, or delving into the truth of the arts… and the truth of my own soul.

Further, this reason has expanded so that I want everybody to study the martial arts, to find the profound joy in the arts that I have found.

My reason may not be yours, and that is okay.

But, whatever your reason, it is yours. Keep looking until you can find it, until you can verbalize it. Until it becomes you.

You won't find the truth of yourself, and you won't find the truth of the martial arts, until you can find out why you study the martial arts.

Or put the martial arts aside and find something else that is closer to the real truth of you.

Chapter Three
Enlightenment

Enlightenment means 'into the light.' It is when somebody gains understanding and clarity regarding something. Sometimes it is a bolt of lightening, more often it is the gradual accumulation of knowledge that elevates one to a superior viewpoint.

A sixth grader is definitely enlightened when compared to a first grader.

That understood, I am about to enlighten you as to the truth of the martial arts.

Somewhere in the next 90 or so pages you're going to see what I'm talking about, and your mind is going to change. It will expand to grasp the concepts I am about to share, and the Martial Arts that you are doing are going to make more sense, and your whole life is going to make more sense.

This is really powerful stuff I am about to tell you.

So hold on to your hat and here we go.

There's a guy, and he is going along, working, having fun, has a few friends, and so on. He's probably pretty much like you and me.

Except that when he goes home and turns on the computer, he dials in some porn.

Now, an interesting thing happens. He has wild images and compulsions in his head.

Before he did that, before he went looking for porn, he didn't. He had an idea, maybe a few sparks, but not the full blown forest fire.

Now he does.

So here is the point: we walk through life looking for experiences. For sensations. For feelings. For emotions.

That is actually the point of this universe. This universe is a big theater in which we have existence. This universe is nothing but a place in which to have our existence, and to experience life.

And the truth of the matter is that we create our own experiences, we choose what to dial in on the internet, in our education, in our lives, and therefore we are responsible for our lives.

Go on, look around, find something that you aren't responsible for.

Even if somebody doesn't like you for no good reason, you may not be at fault...but you are certainly responsible.

Even if an asteroid fell out of the sky and struck you - cosmic 'coincidence,' - you were responsible for choosing to stand in that place at that time.

Chapter Four
Enlightenment Part 2

I want you to think about something.

If you are that guy who is walking down the street, waiting for porn to strike him, or whatever, then you are a victim of this universe. You don't have an idea — you are waiting for one.

The point here is that you have to have some idea of where you are going in life. There has got to be some reason or purpose for what you are and are doing.

Some people have this idea before they are born. They come into life, and everything they do is aimed at a specific 'role,' or even an event, and they know what they are doing. They know their purpose in life.

Many people come into life and don't have a clue as to why. But by the time they are a couple of years old they have formed an idea of where they are going. They know that they are going to be a cop, or a writer, or play some other role.

They have an idea, they have selected what their existence in this life is going to be about.

They know what experiences they wish to experience.

They know what feelings they wish to experience.

They have a sense of themselves and they are on the way. A little late, but on the way.

Some people don't have a clue as to why they are here. Not at all. They didn't have a thought before they were born, their formative years were wasted, and they are the flotsam and jetsam of this life. They drift from job to job, get drunk or drugged (a form of unconsciousness to protect them against the idea that they don't know what they are doing or why), they commit crimes, and they go through life in protest, fighting life at every step of the way.

Poor souls.

This all understood, the fact of the matter is that the universe reacts to our thoughts, and if we put out bad thoughts it creates bad lives, for others as well as ourselves.

And if we put out good thoughts, do good things, then good things happen to us, and to those around us.

An enlightened person does good things. Indeed, true enlightenment may result from this as much as anything else.

Don't feel enlightened? Do good things. It will come to you. This is an absolute.

Chapter Five
Extra Data

Let me give you some data that, though it may appear unrelated, will definitely change you, and help you to achieve enlightenment.

You can't have two thoughts at once.

If you have two thoughts, or more, you are actually having one thought, holding the other thought(s) in place. On 'automatic,' as it were. You can have an AMAZING amount of secondary automatic thoughts.

You can have two thoughts in sequence, and so fast it seems that you are having two thoughts, but you are not.

You simply can't generate two thoughts at once.

Out of this whole dichotomous (two sided) universe you are a 'singular' entity.

And, that understood, there's a 'part two' to this concept: if you are putting out a thought, you can't receive a thought. And the opposite is true: if you are receiving a thought you can't put out a thought.

Yes, you can speak at the same time as someone else, but in that event you won't hear what the other person says, except as an afterthought, a memory, if you will.

Two people speaking simultaneously, two people 'thinking' at each other, results in static, a collision of waves, garbage.

A fellow who has experienced enlightenment, and this will be you as soon as you accept and embrace this concept, will see this, will have it be part of him.

Further, he will experience space, his mind will slow down and shut up, and he will experience thoughts as unique, little experiences.

And these thoughts will all be singular.

You will not have two thoughts at the same time.

You will not be able to give/receive thoughts at the same time.

That is just the truth of you.

And knowing this will go a long way towards helping you generate only good thoughts. After all, when you see the value of your own thoughts you aren't going to be so willing to waste your uniqueness creating bad effects.

The fact is that so many people try to do more than one thing at a time, are compulsed to try and do more than one thing at a time, that they can't understand that the process that leads to enlightenment is to do one thing at a time, to focus their thoughts until they do only one thing at a time.

To get rid of the distractive and disruptive process of trying to do more than one thing at a time.

Chapter Six
Matrixing

The original Matrixing consisted of long lists of techniques written by myself.

I would learn an art, try to combine it with another art, try to combine the techniques, and write a list of the techniques.

The number of techniques would invariably be in the hundreds, and I filled notebook after notebook with these lists.

It was the Golden Age of Martial Arts, you see, and I was being swamped by art after art. Karate and Wing Chun and Aikido and Kung Fu and Bruce Lee and Chuck Norris and all the different magazines and books and then videos…I was swamped.

And, I don't recall exactly when, I began just writing matrixes to contain the vast number of techniques written on the unwieldy lists building in the mounting stack of notebooks.

I tried my hand at making my own art back in the 1980s. It was mostly a combination of this and that, and I didn't really have any original thoughts, I was just overloaded and spitting stuff out.

And I called this art 'Robot Karate.' Good name, for I was 'roboting' what I had absorbed.

Still, I was also 'unroboting.' For in writing things down, in teaching, I was opening myself up and divesting myself of the influences that had pretty much iron bound me.

And the name of the art shortly became 'Matrix Karate.'

It was a far cry from the eventual concise course I would write for Monster Martial Arts, but it was pretty good, too.

And I researched the name 'Matrix.'

A Matrix is a word used to describe a cage used to hold a female wolf for breeding purposes. Matrix comes from 'mother.' And I wanted to present the concepts of the 'mother art.'

Proud fellow, I was, but then sometimes you have to shoot high if you are going to get anywhere.

The matrix I use is a graph used in Boolean Algebra. Boolean Algebra is used to represent three dimensional motions on a two dimensional surface. Thus, concepts used to generate space flight and intricate motions on computers can be used to align concepts in the mind of a human being.

You will see this concept of Matrixing in a later chapter of this book.

At any rate, using matrixes allowed me more freedom, and I began to inspect the martial arts as a science.

Now, this all tells you about Matrixing, and how I developed it, but it doesn't tell you where it comes from.

My father was an engineer who loved to play golf.

When I was growing up the magazines sitting on the end tables were such as Popular Mechanics, and Golfing magazines.

These are the magazines I was weaned on. I would pour over them, reading about such futuristic inventions as cars that fly, telephones you could actually carry around with you, energy direct from the sun, and so on.

I particularly liked the illustrations.

And, I really liked the illustrations in the golf magazines.

I would see men standing in pose, golf club at some point in the swing, with geometrical depictions of planes and arcs, explanations of stress points, and so on.

It was these magazines that shaped me. I never became an engineer, and while golf is cool, it is certainly not the monkey on my back. But the concepts worked in the martial arts.

Martial Arts are the monkey on my back, that and writing.

Writing because my mother was an English teacher, and my grandmother was a Latin teacher, and because it was in that direction that my mind seemed to gestate.

That said, you are the recipient of my invention, and you can approach Matrixing from any viewpoint.

Be you a teacher, an engineer, a cop or whatever…matrixing will make sense, and it will open up and align concepts that have been hiding from you.

When you use a Matrix all the data is presented, and nothing can be hidden.

Oddly, I think this sometimes scares people.

Chapter Seven
Neutronics

In 1974 I had a realization:

For something to be true the opposite must also be true.

This was the birth of neutronics. This was the moment, verbalized, in which I realized the truth of the universe.

I know, it sounds like gibberish, but it actually is a profound thought which borns the universe.

First, consider that it perfectly describes the yin yang symbol.

That said, let's discuss how this concept can describe the universe.

A basic motor consists of two terminals, or poles, between which there is tension. The tension can be push or pull.

Everything in the universe is a motor.

Celestial bodies have two poles, north and south, between which there is tension. This tension causes (balances) such phenomena as gravity and electromagnetism. Thus, a planet such as earth spins, and we don't fall off. And the interchange between the planet's electromagnetism and our own electromagnetism gives rise to life forms.

Every cell has, at its heart, two poles. In a human being these are sodium and potassium.

Every atom has two parts: the electron and the proton.

What about the neutron?

But the neutron has no substance. No charge, no positive or negative. It just sits there and…watches.

Which is what the spirit of a human being, the 'I am,' does.

Which is the meaning behind Neutronics.

Neutronics is about the 'I am' that watches life unfold; that makes life unfold.

Every object in this universe has a trajectory. A flight path. A flow.

When objects collide we have force.

So this universe consists of force and flow.

When you, the 'I am,' are walking your body down the street, you are engaged in a process of avoiding, or causing collision, or force.

You flow this way and that, and the meetings and greetings, or near misses, or outright combat, occur simply based upon the choices you made concerning your flightpath.

You avoided other objects…or you didn't.

Sometimes the collisions are pleasurable. Sometimes not. But always, they are what you chose.

Everything that happens to you in this universe is based on your simple choice.

Somebody punched you on the nose? You made a decision.

Somebody missed you? You made a decision.

An asteroid fell out of the sky and hit you on the head?

You chose to be in that spot at that moment in time. Thus, you are responsible for that collision.

This is all sort of hard for people to accept. It is much easier to plead ignorance, and to continue on the path of irresponsibility.

But everything that happens is because of decisions you made.

Period.

Chapter Eight
Binary

So let's talk about how the universe works, and how you actually function; let's consider the process of adjusting your flow so as to create, or not create, force.

This universe is nothing but objects which flow. Everything is an object, and everything has a path upon which it moves.

So, leaving that alone for a moment, let's talk about what Binary actually is.

In mathematics Binary refers to a system of numbers consisting of only 0 and 1.

2 through 9 are tossed.

So to count to ten you only say, 0…1…10.

And ten is actually three.

Weird, eh?

But pretty useful when you use it to measure the universe.

Consider a light switch. It is either off (0), or it is on (1).

Sounds pretty limited, eh?

Except that morse code is based on off or on, the switch is either down, or up. It is in contact, or it is not. And the whole English language, and a few other languages, are then easily transmitted.

Still, that's pretty lame. I mean, what about colors? Let alone such things as abstract concepts?

Did you know that a computer is based on this concept of 'on or off?' Zero or one?

The computer, because it can deal in larger and larger quantities of zero or one, can describe anything and everything you might want to know.

So let's take this concept of binary, which is the numbers system of the universe, and apply it to the martial arts.

Chapter Nine
Binary Martial Arts

As I said, everything in the universe has a (potential) force and flow.

You walk on to the mat and bow. You face your opponent. He (or you) launch an attack. The attack misses (zero), or succeeds (one).

It can miss in many ways. You can cause it to miss in many ways. You can use a variety of arts, use force or flow, a block or a dodge, but a miss is a miss.
And a hit is a hit.

This is the binary of the martial arts.
This is the reduction of the martial arts to flow, and the potential collision of that flow (force).

Chapter Ten
Force and Flow

All martial arts are based on Force and Flow; all arts are a combination of Force and Flow.

Force can be translated as getting hit, and flow can be understood as being missed.

Thus the martial arts can be described as 'hit' and/or 'miss.'

Karate is pretty much based on hitting or getting hit.

Aikido is pretty much based on making people 'miss you.'

And the various arts are some combination, in some manner of 'hit or miss.'

Wing Chun you make the person miss by 'emptying' (flowing with) the arms.

Tai Chi Chuan you make the person miss by 'emptying' (flowing with) the body.

And so on.

Some arts hit hard, some hit soft, some miss by a little, some miss by a lot.

But all arts are based on growing the variations possible in the concept of 'hit or miss.'

And no art is perfect, or true, because no art ever describes, let alone holds true to, the concept of 'hit or miss.'

No art is based on a perfect understanding and balance of the 'hit or miss' concept.

Chapter Eleven
Basic Binary Variations

When a strike is launched at you you have two choices: to let the punch hit you, or miss you (be guided past, slipped, etc.) And when you launch your strike, it will hit, or it will miss.

Thus: the base techniques of ALL martial arts are, the core concept of ALL martial arts, based on the force or flow concept, are:

'hit or miss.'

A hit is obviously force, and a miss is obviously flow.
Strikes, be they punches, blocks or kicks or whatever, are 'hits.'
Misses are described by guiding, stepping aside, and so on.

So all blocks, strikes, kicks, grabs, throws, evasions, strategies, whole arts, are nothing but variations on the 'hit' and 'miss' concept.

You can describe 'hit' or 'miss' in the following ways.

FORCE	FLOW
Miss	Hit
Pass	Grab
Slap	Stop

And there are more terms.
But even using these terms is a variation on the basic principle. Since you understand that we have now deviated from the truth, however, this is okay. The deviation is small, and we can get away with it and not lose sight of the binary truth of the Martial Arts.

Chapter Twelve
Making the Binary Work

I eventually settled on 'slap/grab' over the other variations of 'hit and miss.' I believe this affords me the best possibility to stay true to the 'hit or miss' concept. Following is a description of how it works.

A strike comes towards you, which is to say an object is proposing to intersect the place you occupy in space.
Your purpose is to force it or flow it.
Or, to use my terminology, to slap it aside, or grab it.

If you let it flow past you, with a slap, or subtle guiding motion, using less and less force as you can, then he will miss. This is the 'Slap' portion of my art.

If you Force it, then you reach forward and 'grab' the biceps. Yes, you could make fist, turn the arm this way or that, and have it be a block, and so on. But to reach forward with the palm and close your hand over the biceps is the 'Grab' portion of my art.

So consider the following graphics.

If you choose to get hit, then you have chosen to occupy a space where the incoming flow intersects the path of your body.

If you move back, then the incoming potential force passes in front of you. You would slap, (or guide) to help the pass.

If you step forward the punch would pass behind you. Because you are inside the other fellows reach (or 'universe') you need to construct a block of some sort.

So there are three potentials on this type of set up:
a hit,
a pass to the punch going in front of you,
a block to the punch going 'behind you.'

Consider these additional viewpoints of these potentials.
SLAP

GRAB

Do you understand what is happening in these two potentials?

The incoming 'missile' passes in front of or in back of.

Since time is a measurement of distance, your sense of time is really an appreciation of space.

Thus, if you don't step aside, or move him aside, you stand at a point of intersection. The fist will hit you.

But if the fist can hit you, you can hit the fist, so to speak, and therein we have the subtle game of adjustment wherein one person seeks advantage over the other person.

Except we are not talking about hitting here, we are talking about grabbing, which is a more likable (to this writer) conclusion for the closure of the fist that is at the end of a strike, or collision of bodies.

GRAB (stop)

SLAP (miss)

Thus, you can slap the attack past, or you can step in and grab it.

Grab it merely by closing your fist on the biceps, or similar portion of the arm.

Yes, you will have to maneuver the body correctly to place yourself in the advantageous position.

But that is the point of it all. To place yourself at advantage, and the other person (terminal) at disadvantage.

Chapter Thirteen
Reversing the Deviation of Martial Arts

I stated earlier that:

Thus: the base techniques of ALL martial arts are, the core concept of ALL martial arts, based on the force or flow concept, are:

'hit or miss.'

Let's examine that so there will be no misunderstanding.

The first time I realized this principle I was doing some teaching, trying to get the student to understand a simple point, and I said:

"A fly is buzzing in front of your nose. Would you do a Karate High Block to chase away the fly?"
The student chuckled at the idea.
"No," I said. "You would slap at it with your hand."
And I made a motion across my face.

The point of this simple conversation was to encourage the student to use a cross body palm block to set up a high block, or any other block.
You can see the precise lesson if you look at the 'House' form, which is presented in Matrix Karate.

In my mind I was seeing more than the House form, however. I was looking at Force and Flow, and working on the 'slap/grab' principle.

The slap was too easy, and there wasn't any where to go with it. But then I realized that the grab was key to my visualization.
I visualized the sequence on the next pages for the 'grab,' or the 'stop' part of my force and flow cogitations.

First you reach out and press on the biceps.

The art progresses, and instead of reaching out and grabbing, you extend the arm and 'override' the incoming punch.

The art progresses, and you execute a karate block.

And the Karate block may become stylized into a kung fu type of block.

It should be said that the sequence of art is not necessarily karate to kung fu, it could be kung fu to karate, or some other art.

In any case, as the student learns stylized movements, he/she loses sight of the simple reach out and stop motion that is inherent in the 'grab' concept.

And, this whole thing makes sense, as it is easier, sometimes to teach large numbers of people (such as Okinawan school children) to throw up the arm in a   block, rather than go from child to child and explain the fine points of actually grabbing the biceps.

Thus, you can see that if you simplify the art, by matrixing, you can reverse engineer the concepts of modern arts right back to the origins of the martial arts, back to the concept of 'pass/stop,' or, as I prefer, 'slap/grab.

Chapter Fourteen
The Classical Martial Arts

What I have said in this book, this binary matrixing I am telling you of, DOES NOT invalidate other martial arts.

It undercuts them, and thus makes them easier to understand, and thus easier to do.

If you understand how a high block deviates from a 'stopping' move, then things you didn't understand about it will lose their importance and go away.

If you understand how all blocks and passes are deviations on the 'hit' or 'miss' principle, you will be more able to construct effective blocks.

You will understand this once you have had a few days to consider what I am saying here, and to work it around in your mind. You will find that your system suddenly becomes a little easier to do.

Here's a simple analogy for what I am saying here:

Let's say you just discovered that algebra is based on concepts of plus or minus. Would you then stop doing all algebra?

No. There is so much to be learning from the grow of the plus and minus concepts in algebra that we would never consider such a thing.

And the same is true in the martial arts.

Understanding the force and flow principles, as illustrated in such concepts as 'slab/grab,' will merely make your advanced art that much easier to understand, and to do. And the advanced principles will become easier to learn and use.

But, the unfortunate truth is that every martial art has forgotten the root of force and flow, and thus the slap and grab concept reawakens the original concepts, and excitement, for the martial arts.

Chapter Fifteen
The Dividing Line

From the last chapter, and understanding that every martial art is a deviation on this 'force or flow/'stop or hit' concept, we should ask ourselves one simple, but important, question: what is the dividing line between slap and grab; at what point, or how, do we know which of these concepts to use?

No matter how neat, or tweaked, or wild a block or strike is…it is a stop. And the shape of the arm and the hand and the body behind it is still nothing but a variation on hitting.

And the same holds true for the flow side of the art, or the miss.

Whether you use the slap or the grab depends on a line drawn down the body. If the strike is on one side of the line it is going to be a hit. If it is on the other side of the line it is going to be a miss.

Consider the following graphic.

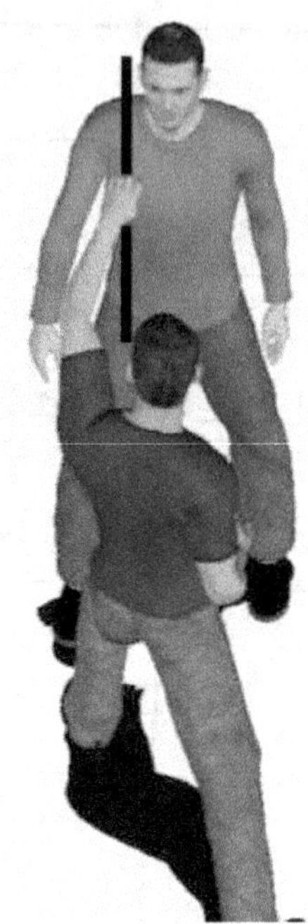

If the strike is on the right side, the head side, of the defender, he will slap it across, letting it miss.

If the strike is on the left side, the shoulder side, of the defender, he will stop it.

The line is pretty well set in stone, but you will have to practice it until it is intuitive.

Interestingly, this opens up an interesting concept.

When you play tennis you don't hit to the forehand, or the backhand, you try to hit it to the dividing line, the place where the receiver can't make up his mind as to which direction he will go.

Chapter Sixteen
The Alley

The beautiful thing about understanding this concept of the Dividing Line is that you can control it by controlling the distance between you and your opponent.

And, even juicier, is the fact that you can control which side of the line an opponent attacks, enabling which type of defense you use, a slap or a grab, simply by holding your hands up as an 'alley.'

Holding them narrow and he will go around.

Hold them wide and he will go through.

Chapter Seventeen
Extrapolating the Grab

Before we proceed, I should point out a few things a Grab has potential for.

In the following illustration, I know it is hard to see, the fellow grabbing the biceps is extending his right thumb.

By doing this he is able to insert his thumb between the muscles in the upper arm. If he was grabbing the shoulder, he could insert his grip into the muscles of the shoulder. And, if he was grabbing the elbow, the forearm, the wrist, or even the hand, he could be inserting his grip into radial nerves, the funny bone, or whatever. These insertions can result in pressure point takedowns, or manipulations which result in throws and locks.

I mention this just to show how the grab can grow into other concepts, and to show how it can be extrapolated into the techniques of classical martial arts.

That said, let's continue with Matrixing the binary.

Chapter Eighteen
A Matrix of Counters

After you block, or make the opponent miss, you will have four potential counters.

The four things you can do are:

Kick
Punch
Knee
Elbow.

Yes, there are more, things you can do. There are types of punches and knees and so forth, and you must be free in your thinking so you can choose and adapt and so on.

BUT…let's just keep it simple and let you develop your art on your own.

Keep it simple by just doing the 'slap,' or the 'grab,' then countering with each of the four techniques. Thus, the matrix looks like this:

	Slap	Grab
Kick		
Punch		
Knee		
Elbow		

The list from this matrix looks like this:

Slap and Kick	Grab and Kick
Slap and Punch	Grab and Punch
Slap and Knee	Grab and Knee
Slap and Elbow	Grab and Elbow

What kind of kick? Depends on the situation and what you prefer, on what will set up the next technique.

Horizontal Elbow or Vertical Elbow? Depends on the situation and what you prefer; on what will set up the next technique.

Grab Arts? They have already been fully matrixed and are introduced in Blinding Steel, and organized and completely defined in Matrix Kung Fu (Monkey Boxing).

And, you will find, in Matrix Kung Fu, that each position of the body calls for a precise selection of Grab Arts, and that when this selection is mastered your Grab Arts will work on Intention, which is to say, 'the least effort for the most effect.'

The point here isn't to tell you exactly how the art is, but to present the basics in such a way that they are simple, will evolve, and yet will also polish so that effective basic-basics can be used.

Thus, you have eight basic techniques, as listed above.

You are free to play with them, sort through various stances and positions and see how to make them work.

Chapter Nineteen
Basic-Basics

I cover the Basic-Basics in every book I write. It is because they are that important. It is because so many schools have ignored them, which has resulted in wholesale degradation of the art.

The Basic-Basics are the underlying foundation to all body motion. They are:

Breath
Relax
Sink Downward
Align the Body
CBM (Coordinated Body Motion)

Sometimes I put CBM in it's own category, and this because it is often the result of, or results from, making the first four items work.

To breath is the basic binary motion of the body. All motion should be aligned with the breath. Breath out when you expand the body. Breath in when you contract the body. Breath out when you strike, or are struck.

Relaxing makes the martial arts work. Yes, focus is important, and in the beginning one grips the fists tightly. But in the end one should be hitting with relaxed fists, sticking the bones of their body through the water of the attaching body without much thought, and especially without effort.

The body is either tight or loose (Force or Flow). It is easy to become tight, the universe trains us to love force because it keeps hitting us in the head. But the real martial arts occur when somebody gets over this universal reaction to impact from the universe and becomes able to relax oneself in the face of force.

Sinking downward makes the body into an efficient machine, and starts the body on the route to generating energy.

Aligning the body is learning how the body actually works, is actually making the body work by studying such things as physics, geometry, and so on.

CBM is when you move the body as one unit. All parts start at the same time, and all parts stop at the same time. All parts move in the same direction, or support a single intention.

Do the basic/basics with every technique, with every move you do.

For instance, do the eight basic techniques, focusing on the first basic/basic.

Then do the eight techniques focusing on the second basic/basic, and so on.

After a few times through you will find that the basic/basics come together, and you will be manifesting MUCH power, and the techniques will be doing nothing but becoming simpler, and even more intuitive.

Chapter Twenty
Matrixing Two Punches

Let's set up a basic matrix for two strikes.

There are four potential strikes here. Here is the matrix:

	right	left
right	right/right	right/left
left	left/right	left/left

These list out, for instance, as:

right punch followed by a right punch
right punch following by a left punch
left punch followed by a right punch
left punch followed by a left punch

I have listed the matrix with punches, but punches are not the only possible attacks. The attacks can be varied, jabs or spins or kicks or whatever, but they still depend on the right/left.

Thus, keeping it simple, we limit everything to these four possibilities, and it is easier to analyze, and to remember, and thus everything will become intuitive.

Don't think in terms of the complexities, just think in terms of right and left, and everything will be easy squeezy, and the terribly chaotic act of fighting will become a binary simplicity.

Chapter Twenty-One
Matrixing a Combination

So let's take just the right/left combination (you can draw a matrix for the other combinations on your own) and draw a matrix for handling it.

	slap	grab
slap	slap/slap	slap/grab
grab	grab/slap	grab/grab

When the right punch comes whistling in, followed by the left, there are only four techniques that you have to learn. They are:

Slap the right past and then slap the left past.
Slap the right past and then palm strike (grab) the left biceps.
Palm strike (grab the right biceps) and then pass the left.
Palm strike (grab the right biceps) and then palm strike (grab the biceps) the left.

Thus, a combination is no longer a hopeless and endless variety of potential blocks and potentials strikes, but rather a simple 'either or' choice. And having an only 'either or' choice is going to make things incredibly simple for the student, and he will need, literally, only one tenth the time to pick up on how to handle combinations.

Which strike do you do? To answer that draw a matrix of potential strikes, go through the potentials, and figure out which ones work. Once you do that you'll never have to think what to do, the logic will propel you.

On the following pages I have illustrated the techniques. Please note that while dealing with four combinations might entail multiple techniques with all sorts of variations in classical martial arts, in this system there are only pass and grab, and, at this point, a matrix of kick, punch, knee, and elbow.

Complexities come later.

And, interesting to note, if you learn in this binary fashion you will find that the extrapolations leap out at you; you will intuitively come up with the next move in the system, as opposed to having somebody laboriously detail and explain it all to you.

You become the artist, not the canvas for someone else to paint upon, but the creator of the art itself.

Slap/Slap for a right/left attack

then counter with a kick/punch/knee/elbow.

Slap/Stop (Grab) for a right/left attack

then counter with a kick/punch/knee/elbow.

Stop/Slap for a right/left attack

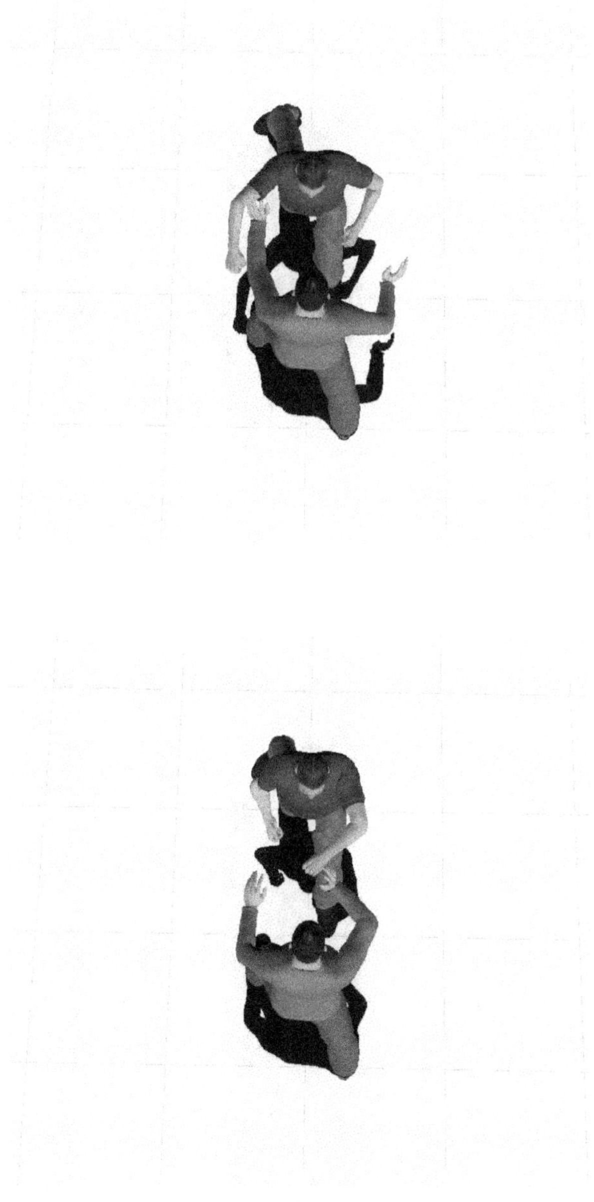

then counter with a kick/punch/knee/elbow.

Stop/Stop for a right/left attack

then counter with a kick/punch/knee/elbow.

Thus, there are only four combinations using
only the binary of miss or hit (slap/grab).

The combinations can be done on either side, and with a variety of counter strikes.

They are VERY simple, easy to remember, will become intuitive VERY fast, and totally combat applicable.

Go on, make a list of techniques and see how many actual techniques you are dealing with to become extremely combat proficient.

And, I would like to add a note at this point. The closest I have ever found to a binary matrix in all the martial arts is found in the forms Sanchin and Seisan. When the old guys made those arts they were hot on the trail of Matrixing.

Unfortunately, they didn't have the physics to describe what they were doing. They understood intuitively, but only eventually and after many years of practice, not in the short period of time it will take you.

Chapter Twenty-Two
Matrixing More Combinations

So will the fellow do more than punch/punch you? Will he kick/kick you? Or punch/kick you?

Here's a matrix for basic combinations.

	punch	kick
punch	punch/punch	punch/kick
kick	kick/punch	kick/kick

Each of these potential combinations can be further matrixed by drawing a 'right/left' matrix for each of the combination.

And you can even get into matrixes for things like hooks and spin fists and types of kicks and all that. But, just so you know, I did already do some of that in the book 'Matrixing Kick Boxing,' and in some of the other books/courses I have written.

The thing that is nice about all this is that even though you are dealing with the complexities of combinations, nothing ever truly gets complex because the fellow is either on the inside or the outside, simplifying the problem into an intuitive response. Believe me, intuition will become the norm shortly after exploring these matrixes I am giving you here.

The point is that drawing a matrix makes the complex into the simple.

You can expand the matrix to include elbows or knees, or whatever you want, even bites and gouges, or other types of specific strikes.

Though you will find that I usually handle a lot of this, especially in some of the courses, by simply matrixing the potential angles of attack.

The main course I do it in, however, is called Blinding Steel, and I will tell you about that course shortly.

Chapter Twenty-Three
A Little Review

Let's do a little review. I know I have given you a lot of data, so let's lay it out and examine it and make sure it really is simple.

An attack can be forced (stopped) or flowed (slapped aside).

A counter can exist of four basic responses, kick, punch, knee and elbow.

There are four potential attack combinations: right/right, right/left, left/right, and left/left.

Put together with four potential defenses, this gives you 16 basic techniques.

The list of attacks or counters can be expanded by adding variations on the attack or defense.

Chapter Twenty-Four
What You are Really Doing

Philosophically, and logically, you are establishing a binary universe. Everything is based on Force and Flow, and the extrapolation of that simplicity is in the hit or miss, the slap or grab, and the matrixing to uncover the potentials for each motion.

Technically, you are exploring hit or miss, matrixing them logically so they expand simply through the potentials of motions.

Matrixing counters, matrixing combinations, and preparing yourself for the next course, the one that matrixes weapons and grab arts.

Thus you are growing an art here. And you will find that as you do this, especially as you practice the material here, not just read and think you understand it, but get a friend and actually work through it, that this material drastically changes the way you look at your martial art.

You are growing the art from a simple seed (binary), into a shoot (hit or miss, slap and grab), into a simple branch (combinations), into finer branches (more complex combinations).

So this means the death of the classical, right? NOT A CHANCE!

What it does is open the door to the other arts, to the methods of thought that the ancient fellows were following when they put their arts together.

Every art has a reason for being, specific purposes behind it's generation and evolution. Every art must be explored for the multiplicity of concepts, for the matrixing of these concepts.

In this way, this method of rendering all arts to binary, and then regrowing them, all the arts will become one.

There is a fellow in Japan believing in zen and ancient spirits.

There is a fellow in America teaching at a strip mall for bucks.

There is a fellow in China learning for competition and trophies.

They are all branches the same tree! The same 'binary martial arts' tree!

Matrix it, analyze what the martial arts are logically, and you will find that people have made choices from the same questions. Wouldn't you like to know all the choices? What people came up with as an answer for a problem posed in an entirely different environment?

Guaranteed, it will make your art better. The more you know the more you can focus on what you need to do to make your art pure, to become true to the 'tree' of the martial arts.

The more arts you have to matrix, the more pure will become your binary viewpoint of the arts, and of all life.

Chapter Twenty-Five
Martial Arts Family Tree

This is a sample tree. Why don't you make one listing all the arts you studied?

Then, make another one with all the martial arts there are.

Fill in blank spaces I may have left, arts I may not have included, and fix any sequences or lineages I haven't listed properly.

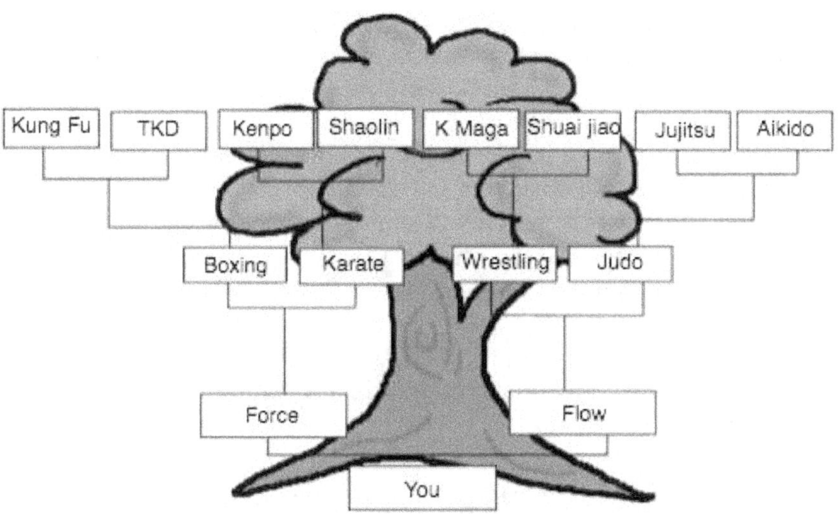

Here's the way the martial arts tree should look.

Again, write your own tree, including all the arts you have studied.

Write a tree with all the martial arts.

Find blank places where you need to study additional arts.

Chapter Twenty-Six
Down the Rabbit Hole

I'm about to go into the original realization that brought me to Matrixing and Neutronics and this method of Force and Flow that you have just been introduced to.

This is hard core theory, and it may seem a little looney to you.

I suggest you put aside any conceptions or expectations and prepare yourself.

Or, perhaps I should say…'unprepare' yourself.

Relax. Take a deep breath.

Here we go.

I have studied Karate, many styles of Karate, and a lot of other martial arts, for nearly 50 years. This is an astounding number of hard blocks; blocks in which I thrust out the arm and close the fist in a hard, snapping motion.

In that time, I have never used a hard block in a fight. Not on the street, and not in freestyle occurring in the dojo.

That's fifty years of practicing something that I don't use.

Are you willing to accept that as a fantasy on some level?

The fantasy of me doing these moves to beat somebody up, when they don't work?

The fantasy in my mind of beating somebody up with these moves that don't work, and are never used in a real fight?

Are you?

And can you apply that to yourself?

Okay, here's the interesting thing: Even though I understand this, I will never stop doing these forms.

The reason is that they exercise the muscle/motors of my body, teach me how to relax and use the body as a machine.

And all that work disciplines my mind so that I am able to do without the distractions of the universe.

And, yes, I get better at self defense, but I get even better at seeking the truth of myself.

This is true for virtually all systems.

Yes, you can use some systems better than others, and there are certain systems that are more 'real' than others. But even when the techniques work, there is still a fantasy aspect, as techniques must be altered for real life punches and kicks and holds and locks.

So, on some level, are you willing to accept the martial arts as a fantasy?

I hope so, because I am about to make them real, we are about go back to Kansas, Dorothy.

I began the martial arts in 1967. I studied hard, absorbing everything I could, and in 1974 I had an experience. The world glowed, and I had a thought.

For something to be true, the opposite must also be true.

I know, sounds a bit like gibberish.

But it was real for me, and truth was, as paraphrased in the movie 'The Matrix,' I wasn't here to make a decision, I had already made the decision, now I had to understand the decision.

Substitute the word 'thought' for 'decision,' and you may understand what my life became like after having my thought.

Now, the following realizations occurred to me over the years; here is a simple list...

This thought, 'For something to be true the opposite must also be true,' was a perfect verbalization, the only verbalization I have ever heard, of the yin yang symbol.

I realized that the universe is nothing but objects having direction (I usually refer to direction as 'flow,' but we are just talking 'trajectory here.'

I realized the purpose of the martial arts, to deliver a force or flow while not receiving a force or flow.

And the way you do this is by analyzing and handling force and direction.

I realized that the universe was dichotomous, that everything came in 'twos.' Front and back, left and right, up and down, inside/outside, and so on.

I began to organize my martial arts in accord with these principles. Techniques had to work on both sides. No poser techniques (where the dummy waits for the defense to be concluded). The body had to be perfectly represented on both sides, and so on.

These realizations, and so many more, were hard won over many decades. Mine isn't an 'add water' story.

But I had them, and I implemented them, and I began to make sense out of the martial arts.

Eventually I stumbled over various matrixing principles, and realized that the martial arts were a science.

And, as I accumulated methods and truly examined the martial arts, I began to see the 'blank spots,' the things that people don't usually see, that are considered 'mysterious,' or 'secret teachings.' These things were right out in the open, and once matrixing had formulated, once I started using the procedure to analyze the various martial arts, they were downright easy to see.

I want to emphasize something here: the thumbnail you have just read is just the briefest, barest of outlines. It is just the shadow of n outline. What you have read I have spent years describing in many, many books.

At any rate, using matrixing a variety of arts have been dissected, analyzed, put back together, to become the fastest and most efficient 'styles' of art in the world.

I say 'style,' but what I am doing with matrixing is creating the pure version, in many cases, of the arts. It is the classical methods that are the styles; they are the deviations and variations. They are the strange growths stemming from the pure and simple truth.

The simple proof for this is that when somebody learns a classical martial art they travel through confusion, and it takes decades.

But when you learn matrixing you travel through resolution, everything falls in place, and it takes months. If that.

If you have done this book on Binary Matrixing, and I mean not just read it looking for ideas and giddy feelings, but done it and examined through the good work of fist on flesh, then you already possess the proof.

You are the proof.

Now, that all understood, I just want to highlight the three most important facets of this list of discoveries I have made.

Here is the original concept which I had back in 1974:

**For something to be true,
the opposite must also be true.**

Applying this to the martial arts, you must assess the path of the fist in regards to it intersecting with your chin. Thus, the purpose of the Martial Arts:

**The purpose of the martial arts is to avoid a force or flow
while delivering a force or flow.**

The method by which we realize the purpose of the Martial Arts:

To analyze and handle force and direction.

Which leads us to the martial arts formula that guides all our actions:

If the force is greater flow it, if the flow is greater force it.

These concepts, these principles, are where my studies originated from. They are where such things as the subjects I label binary matrixing, and matrixing, and neutronics came from.

The only question now is where are you going to go with them.

Chapter Twenty-Seven
The Next Step

Maybe you've been studying the martial arts for a short time, maybe a long time. Maybe you're a youtube aficionado, or you've practiced a dozen different martial arts over the decades.

But no matter where you're at, you can learn more.

The point of matrixing is not to stifle any art, or make less of it, but the contrary; the point of the martial arts is to simplify, make logical, and therefore enable you to make sense of your martial arts, and to learn more martial arts, and to learn them faster.

Consider the word 'intuition.'

Intuition means to grasp a concept instantly, without thinking about it.

It's when the baseball player takes off 'at the crack of the bat.' No thought. Just do.

Classical Martial Arts get you there. They take the person who thinks about things, and makes him into a person who deals with things instantly.

The problem is that the classical martial arts take too long. And they aren't reliable. They don't always work. In fact, they work less and less as time goes on. And the reason for this is that people are being taught about a tree, and are having to work their way through vast, bushy limbs, and never see the seed, the idea that started it all. They can't find the trunk and crawl down to the roots.

In this book you've got the idea, and you're going to find out that your martial arts are different, and that you can become an intuitive person a lot easier and faster than in any other method in the world.

So let's talk about this idea about intuition and intuitive martial arts, and what you should be studying to get there.

In the beginning I wrote eight courses on Matrixing. These are great courses, and they tell you all about matrixing, and how to fix your art, any art that you study, and make it fast and intuitive.

Then I wrote some extra courses, specialty courses on Chi and punching, and the history of the martial arts from a techniques and form point of view.

And, I wrote course I called Blinding Steel.

Now many of the arts I have designed are perfect. Or they provide a viewpoint to perfection of specific areas of the martial arts.

But Blinding Steel is the most perfect martial art I have created.

It isn't an attempt to fix other arts, but a creation of my own. It is perfect from the ground up.

If you do it you can master the martial arts in a few months.

My problem was that I didn't realize what I have done. And, I didn't provide a proper entry into the art. I went right into taking weapons away and disarming and the whole thing.

In writing this book I have provided entry.

And, there is another book, Matrixing Tong Bei, which provides even more data so that you can easily enter Blinding Steel.

If you want the same perfection, the binary concepts, made into totally workable martial arts, martial arts that result in enlightenment and huge human beings, then you need to look at my book on Tong Bei, and then at the Blinding Steel video course.

And this is how you skip to the gravy, if you don't want to waste a lot of years, even decades, and not get to the truth of the martial arts, to the truth of your own intuition.

If you want to fix your martial arts, to get the whole picture, then take the series of eight Matrixing courses.

If you want to get everything I have, all the knowledge, all the research, everything, then you should go to:

MonsterMartialArts.com

The Way of the True Martial Arts
ALL of the courses

The largest and most complete collection of pure martial arts knowledge in the history of the world.

Matrix Combat
Matrix Karate
Matrix Kung Fu
Matrix Aikido
Master Instructor Course
Black Belt Course
Yogata: The Yoga Kata
Matrixing Chi
Pan Gai Noon
Kwon Bup
Buddha Crane Karate
Blinding Steel
Matrixing: The Master Text

Shaolin Butterfly
Butterfly Pa Kua Chang
Matrix Tai Chi Chuan
Five Army Tai Chi Chuan
Create Your Own Art
Rolling Fists
Black Belt Yoga
The Punch
Kang Duk Won
Outlaw Karate
Temple Karate
The Master Books

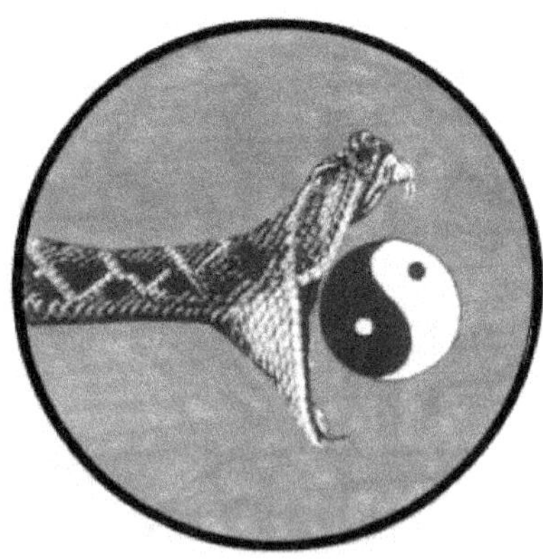

Neutronics

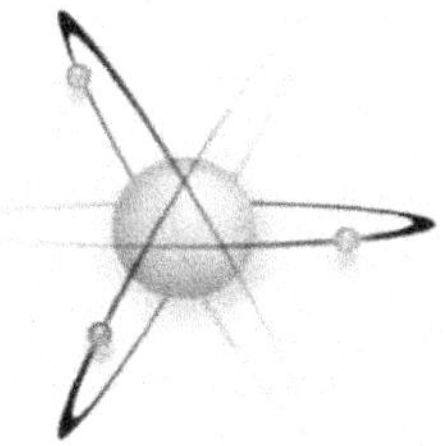

Neutronics is the study of you. It is the study of the 'I am,' the awareness, that motivates the human body. It is born from the martial arts.

When you do the martial arts, especially if you do them in a pure and untainted (matrixed) manner, you will end up with certain questions. Neutronics answers these questions.

Here are the Neutronics books I recommend. They are available at ChurchofMartialArts.com (pdf), and on the internet in paperback form.

The Neutronic Viewpoint
Prologue
Neutronics
Outside the Tube

The Neutronics books have been compiled in one volume:

The Book of Neutronics.

It is available on The internet.

A History of Matrixing
(An encyclopedia of Form and Technique)

A record of Martial Arts research, based on forms and techniques and not a bunch of histories that might or might not be true.

Pan Gai Noon ~ The karate that came fro China and started a major branch of Karate.

Kang Duk Won ~ probably the purest form of karate as it was originally taught to the Okinawan Imperial bodyguards.

Kwon Bup ~ A linear approach to Karate. One fo the most powerful Karates in existence.

Outlaw Karate ~ Synthesizing pure karate out of different systems.

Buddha Crane Karate ~ the first example of Matrixing as applied to Karate.

100 years of Karate as it evolved.
Available on internet. More info at MonsterMartialArts.com

Yoga for Martial Artists

Arranging Yoga according to belts

The oldest exercise system in the world, refined and made logical so that it doesn't sometimes result in enlightenment, but always.

Instead of nibbling away at postures one at a time, the student disco vers the totality of the method, and finds the light at the end of the tunnel.

Available on internet. More info at MonsterMartialArts.com

Changing Karate into Tai Chi Chuan

CHIANG NAN

The original forms of Karate, as 'reverse engineered' through Matrixing. Translates Karate into Tai Chi Chuan. Changes the hard energy of Karate into the soft 'chi' of Tai Chi Chuan.

Available on internet. More info at MonsterMartialArts.com

The Book of Five Arts
(A study of the original forms that were used to create Karate)

Five different arts that, when studied in sequence, provide the complete picture of the martial arts. No missing pieces, no mysticism. Here is the art, hard to soft, from the bottom up.

Available on internet. More info at MonsterMartialArts.com

Start Your Own Martial Arts School
(Step by step method for sure success)

Author has had many schools, here is the precise method he developed to succeed as a martial arts instructor.

Available on internet. More info at MonsterMartialArts.com

Matrixing: The Master Text
The complete history and theory of Matrixing.

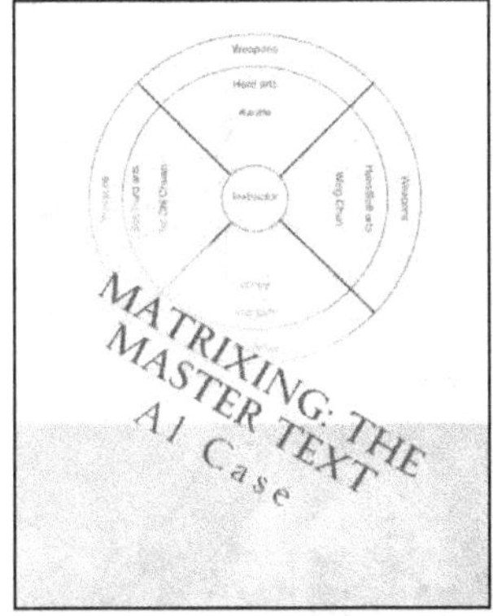

Over 220, full size (8 1/2 by 11) pages. The ULTIMATE description of matrixing. Includes forms and techniques and complete history, including never before seen research into the actual design of the martial arts.
Available on internet. More info at <u>MonsterMartialArts.com</u>

Professional Martial Arts Instructor
The exact knowledge a person needs to teach the Martial Arts

Over 220, full size (8 1/2 by 11) pages, this book is the ULTIMATE instruction on how to be a martial arts instructor. This book is designed to enable ANYBODY to walk into a gymnasium, health club, fitness center, and to present himself as a certified martial arts instructor.
Available on internet. More info at MonsterMartialArts.com

Matrixing Karate
(An encyclopedia of Matrixing)

The greatest Martial Arts innovation in the history of the martial arts. A detailed, step by step understanding of the science of Matrixing. **Available on internet. More info at MonsterMartialArts.com**

THE 'HOW TO CREATE KENPO KARATE' SERIES!

The most incredible analysis of Kenpo Karate in the world.
In depth Matrixing of over 150 Kenpo techniques.
New ways of doing Kenpo forms.
New ways of teaching and structuring classes.
A COMPLETE REWORK OF ONE OF THE MOST
IMPORTANT MARTIAL ARTS SYSTEMS IN THE WORLD!
Over 40,000 words
Nearly 400 pages
Over 800 graphics
Only possible through…

the logic of Matrixing!

Available on internet. More info at MonsterMartialArts.com

The Biggest Martial Arts Lesson of All!

10 volumes, over 150 chapters, over 1500 pages
This massive description of the martial arts takes the reader through the following subjects…

Volume One ~ Origins

Kenpo…Taekwondo…Martial Arts Equipment…Karate…
Kang Duk Won
Where Did the Martial Arts Come From?
The Terrible Truth About Ed Parker
Ed Parker and Bruce Lee were Traitors
The Hellish Beginnings Of Tae Kwon Do
Karate Breaking Technique and a Man's Skull!
Creating The Perfect Body
What Happened to Mess Up Karate!
The Obsession with False Martial Arts Power

AND MORE…

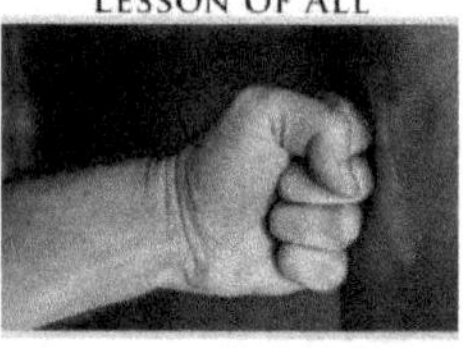

Volume Two ~ Basics

Stances…Punches…Kicks
The Secret Of Chi Power Through The Horse Stance
The Ancient Method for Creating an Iron Grip with Karate!
The Five Parts of a Punch!
Supercharging For The Most Powerful Punch!
How to Knock Out People
Breaking Boards with a Single Finger
Mad Monkey Kung Fu and the Hardest Fist in the World!
The Sneakiest Hardest Kick That Always Works

AND MORE…

Volume Three ~ Forms

Forms…black belt…zen
The Secret Golden Power of Karate
Karate Throws for Fun and Maim!
Setting Up the Flux in Kata Pinan Five
The Sordid Truth About Martial Arts Belt Ranking Systems
What the Training Beyond Black Belt Should Really Be
The Man Who Threw Stones At The Moon
A Very Intriguing Method for Making Martial Arts Chi
How to Get the Gunfighter Mentality in Martial Arts!
Using The Martial Arts To Read Minds

AND MORE…

Volume Four ~ Fighting

Fighting…Weapons

How Bruce Lee Handled Stalking in Classical Karate
The Three Types of Karate Fighters
The Tough and Iron Fists of Old Time Karate!
Five Karate Freestyle Concepts that Win Every Time!
The Three Types of Reaction Time
The Four Decisions of a Fight!
Seven Criminal Reasons to Learn Kung Fu!
Martial Arts and Self Defense Against Weapons
Shoot 'Em Again! It's Only a Stun Gun!

AND MORE…

Volume Five ~ Origins

Weapons…Aikido…Crowd Walking…Kung Fu

Seven Deadly Martial Arts Weapons...One Article of Clothing
Five Knife Fighting Lies in the Martial Arts
Taking the Knife Away from a Slasher in a Knife Fight
Martial Arts Applied to the Five Points of Gun Training
The Value of a Shotgun in Self Defense
Don't Take a Gun to a Martial Arts Fight!
Mystical Aikido Ki Power
Combining Wing Chun and Aikido
Martial Arts Crowd Walking Procedures

AND MORE…

Volume Six ~ Kung Fu

Kung Fu…Masters…Pa Kua Chang…Chi Power

The Real Shaolin History They Wouldn't Tell You!
An Argument Concerning Iron Fist Methods
How to Change Karate into Kung Fu!
Light Body Kung Fu and Walking on Water
The Toughest Karate Master In The World!
Pa Kua Chang, Walking the Circle, and Entering Insanity
The Secret of Pa Kua Chang Is Really Weird
Baguazhang Energy Flux...The Secret Nobody Knows

AND MORE…

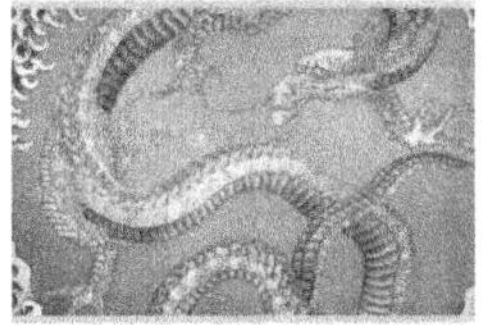

Volume Seven ~ Chi Power

Chi Power…Tai Chi Chuan…Rare Martial Arts…
Yoga…How to Teach Yourself

Five Types of Power One Learns in Martial Arts Flow Theory
The Fabulous and Not To Be Denied Golden Sphere
The Secret of How to Glow with the Martial Arts
The Dangers Of Coiling Power In Pa Kua Chang
Tractor Beams in the Martial Arts
Flux Theory and the Secret of Negative Tai Chi Chuan Chi
Dog Kung Fu Proves Women More Vicious of the Species!

AND MORE…

Volume Eight ~ Matrixing

How to Teach Yourself…Mysticism…How to Teach the Martial Arts…Matrixing

Fighting Devil Dogs Hot and Heavy on Martial Arts
How Much Martial Arts Do You Need?
Gaining Sixth Sense Ability in the Martial Arts
Using Space to Beat your Opponent!
The Four Stages of Mind Over Matter
5 Things I Wish People Would Have Told Me About the MA!
Five Things You Don't Ever Want to Hear in an MA Class
Who Invented the First Martial Arts Matrix?

AND MORE…

Volume Nine ~ Neutronics

Matrixing…Neutronics

Learn Kung Fu by Flipping the Matrix
How and Why Matrixing Works in the Martial Arts!
Learn the Martial Arts Ten Times Faster!
6 Times the Techniques with 1 Simple Trick!
The Motor of the Martial Arts
See Behind Your Head with Simple Karate Trick!
The Third Evolutionary Step Of The Martial Arts
MA Men are Robots, MA Women Don't Get It
Using Neutronics to get Negative Gains in the Martial Arts
The Five Realms of the True Martial Artist

AND MORE…

Volume Ten ~ Odds and Ends

Weird and Odd parts of the Martial Arts

How to Kill a Leopard with Your Bare Karate Hands!
Learn Zombie Kung Fu Now and Kill the Living!
The Brain Crash Behind the Martial Arts
How to Become Bruce Lee Tough
The Greatest Samurai (6 parts)
Why It's Hard to Kill People with Karate or Kung Fu!
A Terrorist, You, and ONE Martial Arts Technique!
Dr. Root's Traveling Snake Oil Kung Fu Lessons
Bruce Lee Workouts and How to Build Real Strength

AND MORE…

The Book of Neutronics
The science behind the science of
Matrixing in the Martial Arts

The philosophy of the Martial Arts made logical through matrixing.

Matrixing is the science of the martial arts, but behind the science is the philosophy. This book finally and totally defines the philosophy of the martial arts.

Available on internet. More info at MonsterMartialArts.com

The Last Martial Arts Book:
Nine Square Diagram Boxing

After 50 years of research and training, this is the end product: a book that sums up the martial arts, ties them all together, in one, simple, easy to learn series of 9 techniques.

Striking, jointlocks, forms, techniques, everything is here.

Nine simple forms on a pattern that encompasses virtually all martial arts, creates a path from hard to soft, and is truly the last, and possibly the only, martial art you will ever need to learn.

Available on internet. More info at MonsterMartialArts.com